When

No One Else

Believed

Praise for: *When No One Else Believed*

Ron's book is a must-read for anyone facing insurmountable obstacles which require a faith that does not look at circumstances but instead focuses on God. I strongly urge you to read this story of Patsy's Miracle for a dose of inspiration.

Dwight (Ike) Reighard,
CEO and President of Must Ministries, Atlanta, GA
Co-author with Zig Ziglar of *Daily Insights*
Tightrope Tango, Treasures from the Dark,
Discovering Your North Star

Throughout the story, Ron was lovingly devoted to Patsy and his belief that God was going to do a miracle. He held onto faith even when there was little else to hold onto.

Sr. Pastor Thomas Cooley,
Cobb Vineyard Church, Kennesaw, GA
www.CobbVineyard.com

I have known Ron for over fifty years. His wife Patsy is the best thing that ever happened to him. It came as no surprise to me that, when she became ill, he would rely on his unwavering faith to see him through... truly an inspirational tale of perseverance against overwhelming odds.

Dennis M. Walsh
NOBODY WALKS, Bringing My Brother's Killer to Justice

Divine Inspiration

One Man's Perseverance

WHEN

NO ONE ELSE

BELIEVED

The Story of Patsy's Miracle

———

RON TRIPODO

RJT Publishing

Author: Ron Tripodo
Cover Design: Robert Ousnamer
Final Edit: Christy Callahan
Staff supplied by EA Books Publishing

ISBN: 978-0578187792

DEDICATION

Violet (Vi) Tripodo

To my mom, the angel who spent so many long nights helping me with my homework. She was a woman who was way ahead of her time. She could do anything.

She was a master chef, a fantastic baker, and a seamstress. My mom could design and make a wedding dress for a bride or a baptismal christening outfit for an infant. She was an artist with a paintbrush on canvas. She could do carpentry, hang wallpaper, or paint the house. She was a support to my father's business, keeping the books and providing customer care.

My mom was "the wind beneath my father's wings." She was the epitome of..."I AM WOMAN, HEAR ME ROAR.

ADHD
FRIENDLY

This book was designed to be an easy read.
The sentence structure, the shorter paragraphs,
the larger print, and the wider line spacing
offer a comfortable and enjoyable
experience for any reader.

FOREWORD

A Nobel Prize winning physicist once stated that he no longer believes the universe is composed of atoms. He now believes the universe is composed of stories. One such story is "When No One Else Believed." It is a true story that will inspire and motivate you to trust God for miracles in your own life.

My good friend Ron Tripodo has written his own story of his wife, Patsy, overcoming overwhelming odds from a medical condition that threatened to take her life. Ron was reduced to knowing that it would not be doctors, nurses, or hospitals that would allow his wife to live... it would truly take a miracle from God.

Ron is very thankful for all the people who helped Patsy on her journey through a health crisis, but, at the end of the day, he knows that it was God who provided the miracle. One of the most amazing facets of Patsy's story is Ron's faith from the time Patsy was in a coma until she recovered. After an event, you often hear people talk about how God came through in a pressure-packed situation and provided a miraculous solution to a problem. Ron, however, gave God glory and honor through a series of billboards proclaiming that God had healed his wife before the healing was complete! Ron's audacious faith is a huge part of Patsy's miraculous recovery.

Ron's book is a must read for anyone facing a mountain of obstacles that will require a faith that does not look at circumstances but, instead, focuses on God. I strongly encourage you to read "When No One Else Believed." to get to know the story of Ron's and Patsy's lives. They are the real deal, they are my friends, and they are passionate believers in Jesus Christ. Their story is one in a million.

In the Master's Service,

Dwight (Ike) Reighard
President & CEO, Must Ministries Atlanta

TABLE OF CONTENTS

INTRODUCTION

Divine Inspiration

N o one ever thinks they will experience a miracle in their lives. We get caught up in everyday living — family, work, friendships, and coping with the everyday stress of the modern world, while still feeling the anguish of past wounds. As we jog along on life's treadmill, it is easy to forget that God is always present, ready with His divine grace and guidance — *if only we would ask... if only we would listen... if only we would trust.*

Who would ever think a day would come when they would be completely traumatized by one single event... an event that happens in an instant that feels like eternity... an event that changes life's course dramatically...an event that brings God's presence into all of life's moments? I've had one of those events.

This story is about that event and about a miracle. Along with it, comes a love story and my awakening to God's will. It is truly Patsy's miracle, but, in a way, it is mine too, because it changed my life so dramatically in many ways. Through the writing of this book, I have come to realize that there is more than one miracle within this story. I have gained a greater understanding of God, and I have experienced His awesome power, His amazing grace, His infinite wisdom, and His unconditional love.

It is my voice you will hear telling the story, sharing my own thoughts and feelings. But God's love and grace living within me have inspired me to write these words. It has been a long, hard journey and a true test of my faith in God, who kept asking, "*Are you going to trust me no matter what?*" It is a question I had to answer over and over again throughout the emotional turmoil of that time.

Many people witnessed this miracle, and many more have read and viewed the videos produced by Channel 2 ABC and the 700 Club that appear on Patsy's website, patsysmiracle.org. Now, many more will know by reading this book.

God is giving us all another chance to receive his grace through this miracle. God wants us to know how much He loves us. He wants us to love Him, and He wants us to love others as unconditionally as He loves us. In Matthew 22:37-40, Jesus spoke His Father's two greatest commandments:

"You must Love the Lord your God
with all your heart,
all your soul,
and all your mind."
AND
"Love your neighbor as yourself."

God wants His people to spread His word. He uses all things for His good and His glory — even a wretched man like me to write, and an unbeliever named Muriel to edit this book. He is the true Author of this book. I was merely the one pounding the keys. Muriel was the one checking the grammar. But He was the One inspiring me with these words.

I can only hope and pray that believers will be strengthened by this story, those teetering on the fence will lean toward God's side, and non-believers will be inspired by the thought of *What if?*...

PROLOGUE

Me, Lord?
You Have to Be Kidding!

I t had been ten years since my wife, Patsy, made her miraculous recovery from an illness that is usually a death sentence. Like the flowers of summer, she had continued to grow and blossom. We were more in love now than ever. But my career path had led to a series of dead ends.

No matter what I tried, I kept slamming into brick walls. My wealth and success went down the chute. I began to feel moments of panic, knowing that Patsy depended on me, and I could not fail. In the past, I had always been able to deal with adversity, pick myself up, and move on. I had the Midas touch in business; things would just "turn into gold." Now I was stuck, spinning my wheels, going nowhere. This had never happened to me before. I was stopped in my tracks every time I started a new venture, and I could not understand why.

It began in September of 2008 when the market crashed. I woke up to find that I had lost over 70 percent of my net worth overnight. I had acquired a large loan for my company, one leveraged against my personal holdings. Now, I no longer had enough equity to secure the loan. So, my bank called their loan, giving me just six months to find another bank.

That's when I met Jim, a Christian brother who was a money broker. We became very good friends. Jim had been working diligently to find me a bank that would buy off and service the loan. He found one, but there was one condition. They wanted to give my bank a haircut — a considerably smaller payoff amount than what I actually owed.

"Thanks, Jim," I said. "I really appreciate you trying to help, but I wouldn't feel right about doing that. I want to pay what I owe. It's the right thing to do.

"But, Ron, let's be realistic," he replied. "Everybody's in the same boat now. Everybody's coming up short. With the economy tanking like it is, the banks are going to have to accept reduced payoffs. They have no choice."

"Jim, I understand, but I just can't do that. I want to pay my debts. That's what God wants us to do. I'll find another way."

Time was running out, and I had to make a move. I found a company that would merge with my company. However, they insisted on owning fifty-one percent of the stock, giving them control. I knew this was not a smart move. Furthermore, the men that were interested in becoming my partners did not seem to share my views on business ethics. I had started to back out of the deal because of that. However, they called me and assured me that I had nothing to worry about in that regard. I was still reluctant, but feared that the bank would call my loan. It overrode my instincts and my will to trust God.

It was not long after the merger that I realized I should have followed my instincts. We had a major clash due to an ethical dispute. Since they had control, they fired me. They had also failed to honor my employment contract. The court battle that followed consumed much of my time and all my remaining money. Although we finally settled, it was not nearly enough to cover my losses.

While that was going on, I took a position with a construction company I had done business with in the past. Everything was going well until I discovered some irregularities in my inventory. Inventory that I had never received was being placed on my books. A red flag went up. When I challenged the records, I was fired without cause.

Then, another company contacted me. They wanted to branch out into the wireless business, so they hired me to build a startup for this division. Within a year, the startup company became very profitable. But once that was accomplished, I had a growing feeling that my role there was about to end. In my mind, I believed that they thought I wasn't needed anymore. The hard work had already been done. Sure enough, promises that had been made to me earlier were broken.

When I confronted them, I confronted them with anger and frustration. My ADHD prevented me from articulating my thoughts calmly to address the situation. I am sure my past dealings with my former partners contributed to fueling some of this anger. I was relieved of my duties.

Nothing like this had ever happened to me before. I had been stopped dead in my tracks no matter what I did. I was baffled. It sure looked like some kind of pattern. Was God trying to tell me something? Whatever it was I sure wasn't getting it.

Once again, I started a new business venture – this time with a partner who was a Christian. I was convinced that this was the business that would seal my future. However, we got into a serious argument over our business contract. After my partner fasted for two weeks, he came back to me and said that God had told him to break up the partnership and give back the money I had invested in the company.

"Yeah, right!" I thought to myself. *"He is using God to steal the company from me."*

Back then, my partner's claim of divine intervention seemed preposterous. But now, as I write this book, I am giving serious consideration to his claim of divine intervention. God can use anyone for His purpose.

We did part civilly. I was not going to fight him. All the fight was out of me from the court hearings I had just been through.

As usual, I had my hearing aid off and my dark glasses on. I've never been a very good listener, and I don't always see what is right in front of me. I was so focused on pursuing my own plans in my own way that I never stopped to think that God might have other plans for me.

After God had blessed us with His miracle, I had done everything I could think of to witness to His name. I told all who would listen about the miracle. I gave our testimony at churches, and Patsy came with me so people could see for themselves what God had done. I used social media, TV and radio commercials, a website, and made other grandiose gestures! What more could he want from me?

They say that news travels fast. So, apparently, did the news that I had parted ways with my partner. Within a few weeks, I received calls from two different companies in my industry — companies that knew me well. They both invited me to come to work with them. I told them I needed some time to think about it. After a couple of weeks, I called them both back to see what my options were and left them messages. I didn't hear back from either one.

Two weeks went by, and I was puzzled. Both companies had seemed so eager to talk to me. So, I called them again, thinking they had not gotten the messages. But I never heard from either of them again.

It was like getting struck by a lightning bolt in a storm. It jolted me with such intensity that it led me to question my whole life and my purpose. Did God want me to come to work for Him? What could he want from me? Was I to become a missionary and go to Africa? Was I to become an evangelist? *Hello*, I don't think so. Wow, was I clueless? I had no idea, but I was going to find out.

After several months of being unemployed and getting nowhere in the job market, I was in a dilemma. I had always felt that God had a purpose for me, but I never knew what it was. As I agonized in idleness, my thoughts kept returning to Patsy's miracle. It had never been written. Not the whole story. Not in a book. And I was the only one who knew the whole story. Did God want me to write it? I kept saying to myself, *"Naaah! It can't be."* But the more I thought about it, the more it haunted me, and the more it haunted me, the more I thought about it.

"Me? Write a book? You have to be kidding me, Lord!" I hadn't picked up a book in forty years and had avoided them whenever possible in my school years. My school years were a disaster. They were so bad that, if I brought home D's, my parents were just relieved that I could get to the next grade.

My mom was an angel. She worked with me almost every night, but to little effect. It wasn't that I didn't try. But back then, no one had ever heard of Attention Deficit Hyperactive Disorder (ADHD), and I had it big-time. I couldn't read well enough to learn from books, and I couldn't focus my attention long enough to learn in class. It was so bad that summer school was just part of my curriculum for my twelve years, or I should say thirteen. I had flunked the third grade. The silver lining on that cloud was that I made life-long friends among my new classmates.

My social life at school was torture. The other kids thought I was dumb, and I was often the butt of jokes. When the other kids took shots at me, I was like a deer in the headlights. My mind just froze. With ADHD, the emotional reaction to the razzing by the kids impaired my capacity to think. My mind was blank. I couldn't process the situation or the language fast enough to think up a quick come-back. What I said, if I said anything, generally made little sense, and only made matters worse.

I had only three options: get mad, suck it up, or walk away. When I got mad I got in trouble. When I sucked it up I felt humiliated. When I walked away I felt like a coward. Needless to say I got in trouble a lot. I was just clueless with no sense of where I was going or how to get there or even why...

One time in the fifth grade, my teacher wanted me to find Ohio on a world map that she had taped to the blackboard. Reluctantly, I walked up to the front and looked at the map, silently praying, "Please, God, just let me be close to where Ohio might be." It was like playing *Pin the Tail on the Donkey* blindfolded. I was searching in Asia up around Siberia. I felt the explosion of silent laughter all around me until, mercifully, my teacher told me to sit down.

The teacher's remark was, "Whatever you do, Ronnie, don't become an air traffic controller."

I thought to myself, "I wasn't that far off. Alaska was pretty close... I think." I pretended not to notice the stifled snickers as I made my way sheepishly back to my seat.

Even after we became adults, my old school friends made jokes about my former scholastic achievements. I have a friend named Dennis who had gone to grade school with me. As adults, we would get together periodically at social events. Dennis had great wit, and he liked to work the crowd, especially at my expense. I was okay with it, or that's what I wanted everyone to believe, so I sucked up and laughed along with the group. The truth is that it always stung a bit. Dennis's wit was out of my league, and I couldn't respond for fear of saying something that would make me look even dumber than I was in his story. At least it kept me humble.

There were lots of Ronnie Tripodo stories that were funny due to my ADHD gaffes... usually brought about by my talking without thinking, a typical ADHD trait exemplified by: "Ready! Fire! Aim!" I provided a library of material for my friends to use for laughs. One of Dennis' favorite one-liners was, "Ronnie did so poorly in grade school that he was the only kid in the eighth grade with a driver's license, a draft card, and a full beard."

Dennis was not being cruel. At the time, I was a highly successful entrepreneur, and I knew that he was complimenting me with his humor. In essence, he was saying that, even with my handicaps, I had managed to accomplish some pretty impressive things. What no one knew was that God had always been by my side, helping me to climb over life's obstacles in spite of my deficiencies.

But now, I was out of work, I was running out of money, and God wanted me to write a book? As they say in New York, "Fuhgeddaboudit!" A book... with my ADHD? I don't think so! My ADHD is like trying to watch sixteen TV screens at the same time. I couldn't sit in a meeting for more than twenty minutes or pay attention to a conversation for very long without drifting away. Even my children could feel the disconnection. I couldn't articulate even simple thoughts or feelings to someone else, let alone write a whole book. I would have a better chance of finding Jimmy Hoffa's grave.

I kept telling God, "I can't write it, Lord. I would if I could. Please forgive me."

I tried to get around it by calling a well-known ghost writer, but I couldn't afford the fee. Neither could I afford to take time off from the job hunt. I was stuck between a rock and a hard place. I could not write this book!

God has a way of knowing who will best serve Him. In the Bible, God chose Paul to become His advocate even though Paul had been responsible for killing many Christians. God knew that Paul's heart would change. God has given us free will and does not intervene unless He knows that we will choose to accept His guidance and His purpose for us.

In this case, God sent a strong message to Paul. He knocked Paul off his horse and subjected him to blindness, starvation, and many other trials before Paul finally understood his purpose. Through God's grace, Paul found redemption, and he was inspired to spread God's word throughout the land and become a great writer of the gospel.

And now, God had made it clear what He expected me to do. As you know, when you get the call, you'd better answer, because the will of God is the strongest force in the universe, and His Will *will* be done. The events of the last decade have convinced me of that.

So I finally said, "Okay, God, I'll do it. I promise. But first I've got to find a way to make a living." I decided then that I had to reinvent myself... fast... but how?

By now you are probably asking yourself how can this guy... who doesn't sound all that bright... who has a massive case of ADHD... who can't articulate well...who can't sit still for very long... and who hadn't even read a book in forty years... be writing this book. Did God miraculously heal him with His supernatural power? No, He chose a different way. He used the next best thing — His creation — man.

When God created us, He gave us the ability to acquire knowledge and skills that we could then use to help ourselves. God can guide the hands of a surgeon to perform with perfect precision. He can guide the mind of a doctor to find the correct diagnosis. He can guide the instincts of the chemist to create the medications needed to cure a disease. In my case, God's solution was a medication – created by chemists, and prescribed by a doctor.

In October of 2015, when I went to my doctor, I told him that I had decided on a new career. I wanted to become a real estate agent, but I was sure I could never pass the test. Dr. Early sat down with me and started asking a lot of questions. Most likely, he already knew that I had ADHD. It stuck out like a sore thumb.

For years, people close to me had complained that I had an attention problem; that I acted impulsively; that I didn't express my thoughts clearly; and that I didn't listen. A trusted employee named Bobbie told me how medication had helped her daughter who had similar behavior. She suggested that I look into it. As usual, I'm not a good listener. I thought to myself, "*Naaah, I don't have that*," and I brushed it off.

Now, to my surprise, my doctor said, "Ron, by your answers to my questions, I can say without a doubt you have a massive case of ADHD."

"Wow!!" So I did have it after all! He prescribed Adderall, a medicine that is often used to treat ADHD in children as well as adults. The doctor said I would know right away if this was the right medicine.

Within a few days my awareness of the world changed dramatically. I discovered that I could now focus on one thing at a time without having my thoughts flit in sixteen different directions at once. I could listen without interrupting and learn from listening. I had the patience to sit and read a book for the first time in my life, and I could begin to comprehend what I read. For the first time, I could articulate my thoughts and feelings without anger and frustration. At last, I began to realize how little I knew and how much I would have to learn. But I also knew that, with God's help, I could do whatever I set my mind to.

I didn't know what a game changer this medicine was going to be! I knew I had the habits of a lifetime to change, but I was determined to do what I had promised God that I would do.

And so I wrote this book.

CHAPTER 1

Our Love Was Being Tested.

T he year 2005 seems a lifetime ago. It was the year before our lives came crashing down on us. It was the year before the miracle. And it was the year that almost shattered our marriage. We had been married for eighteen years. In the past few years, our marriage had started to erode. I think it was a combination of work, blended family, differences of opinion, and a thousand little irritations that met unyielding stubbornness on both sides.

It had been going on for a while. It was pretty much a daily event. We fought at home, at work, even when we went out to eat. We would always leave angry, and the constant fighting was tearing us apart. One source of our problems was that we were a blended family. As anyone who has ever been part of a blended family can tell you, it can be very stressful and a real test of the foundation of your marriage.

Because of our different parenting styles, some of our conflicts were centered on our kids. No matter how hard we tried, we couldn't help but feel closer to our own. When our kids were younger they became adept at playing one of us against the other. We tried to balance love and discipline, tried not to play favorites, tried to set rules that were fair to all. But we often disagreed on how all that should be done. Where was King Solomon back then? Some of this continued even after the kids were grown and it affected our relationships with the grandkids.

All of these things had mounded up, and we began to doubt each other's love. We spent too much time being frustrated and angry at each other. There were times when Patsy thought I didn't love her. I began to think that Patsy didn't love me either. We both became insecure in our marriage. One day she said to me, "If I ever got sick, Ron, you would never take care of me!" Did Patsy have a premonition of how our love would soon be put to the test? Was God sending me a warning?

By mid-spring of 2005, our marriage was at the breaking point. Patsy began going to a Christian counselor in hopes that it would help our relationship. I wholeheartedly supported her decision. I, in turn, took counsel with a good Christian friend. I assumed that Patsy was getting counseling based on the teachings of Christ to help mend our troubled marriage. Was I ever wrong!

Patsy began to confront me with things the counselor had said to her. Apparently, the counselor had been in a bad marriage. There was no forgiveness in her heart, much less the Spirit of Christ. She advised Patsy to leave me, saying that I was just like her own, worthless, ex-husband. Patsy had been prepared to accept the wisdom and advice of this well-recommended Christian counselor; so it was natural for her to assimilate the other woman's anger and resentment. I believe that set the mood for the clash of wills that almost destroyed our marriage.

In mid-June, things came to a head. I can't even remember what the dispute was about, but the argument was very heated, and it started to escalate. We were in such disagreement that Patsy gave me an ultimatum to this effect: "It's either my way or the highway!"

Like snarling wolves, we faced off, and I gave her my answer. "Don't let the door hit you on the way out." And with that, she packed up her clothes and left.

At first, I was glad. But as reality settled in, my heart ached. I couldn't sleep or function at work. Without Patsy, my world was empty; I missed her so much. My thoughts and emotions were in total conflict. On the one hand, I thought she was being unreasonable and stubborn, and I was angry with her. On the other hand, I loved her beyond all reason. My thoughts were in disarray. I raged, I cried, and I prayed.

During this time, I was counseling with a good Christian friend named Kevin. He would say to me, "What is your part in all of this, Ronnie?"

"Kevin, are you crazy?" I replied. "I don't have any part in this! Did you forget? She left me! She's the one who gave the ultimatum – not me!"

And Kevin would say again, "What is your part in all of this, Ronnie?"

I didn't realize then how my anger totally blinded me to my part in the situation. I resented Kevin for not taking my side, but Kevin wasn't afraid to risk our friendship to try to help me. That is a true friend. To Kevin, the wellbeing of our marriage was so important that he was willing to put our friendship on the line. At the time, I thought Kevin was completely nuts. I suspected him of having undergone a clandestine frontal lobotomy. But it was his unconditional love and friendship for Patsy and me that led me to understand what my part had been in our failing marriage.

Two, or maybe three weeks passed, and I thought more and more about what my part in all of this had been. I felt as if my life had just stopped. But the incredible pain I was suffering was only a glimpse of what I would go through later. Perhaps it was God's way of showing me what I was capable of enduring if only I clung to my faith.

I was home, debating what to do, when I heard the chime on the security alarm sound. With my heart pounding, I ran to the top of the stairs and looked down.

There she was. The way she looked at me was the way I had seen her look at me so many times before. It was euphoric. Her eyes said, *"I love you Ron Tripodo."* Her beauty was so radiant that I was mesmerized. I stood there for a second or two in awe. Then I flew down the steps to hold her in my arms. We clung to each other so tightly that we became as one, both of us crying, neither of us saying a word, just holding each other. In that moment, I knew she would always be the only one for me, and I would do whatever it took to mend our marriage and keep her from ever leaving me again.

When all was said and done, what really mattered were not all the issues we had argued about. What mattered were each other — Patsy and me. I think that God was preparing us right then for the test of all tests. He knew we had to be of one heart and one mind to go through the trials ahead. Only then could we show others that God still offers his loving mercy to all who believe in him, regardless of their faults and past sins.

Patsy and I were so immersed in the joy of our reunion that we spoke very little that afternoon. We were just glad to be together again, doing our ordinary, everyday tasks and delighting in each other's presence. That day, nothing felt ordinary, and we seemed to glow in our love.

It was now early July, and our nineteenth anniversary was coming up in a few days. Let me tell you, it was to be one of the most memorable nights of my life.

In the next few days, I was debating what gift to get Patsy. I wanted it to be something special... something that would tell her how much she meant to me. My first thought was a diamond ring to symbolize the renewal of our marriage, or maybe some elegant lingerie to let her know how beautiful she was to me.

I wandered from store to store and found nothing that seemed quite right. I was walking through the mall and stopped at the Hallmark store. I went in and saw a card that just knocked me over — the perfect card that you can never find to express exactly how you feel. On the front was a little boy, shyly holding out a flower to a little girl. That's the way I felt... like a kid again with all that butterfly-happy feeling of being in love. What better gift for Patsy than to show her a close-up of my heart and my love for her!

I had always bought her expensive gifts whether it was a special day or not. But sometimes, for someone to know how much you love them, you want something as simple as a card. The picture, the message inside, and what you write on the card can totally highlight your love without another gift getting in the way. Words can be powerful. It was so simple and so perfect that it said everything. The message inside was, *"You are my everything."*

"You Are My Everything"

On the night of our anniversary, I was waiting for her downstairs, like a groom waiting for his bride on their honeymoon night. Patsy came down the steps wearing an exquisite, white summer dress. A narrow, gold belt streamlined her marvelous figure, and a gold necklace framed her lovely face. She looked like an angel stepping down the stairway from heaven wearing gold high heels that gleamed like Cinderella's glass slippers. I had to catch my breath. At that moment I wanted to be Prince Charming, putting the shoe on her foot and making her my princess.

Patsy had always been beautiful, but that night she looked extraordinary! I just gazed at Patsy, my heart overflowing with love. I could hardly believe that I was actually married to this raving beauty. I felt like the luckiest guy in the world. It brought me back to our wedding day.

I remembered that hot, sultry, summer day in July when we had our wedding outside. I had wanted it to be a day to remember forever. I had a song I wanted to sing that fit so perfectly for the two of us. I looked into Patsy's eyes and sang these lyrics:

Did you ever know that you're my hero,
and everything I would like to be?
I can fly higher than an eagle,
'cause you are the wind beneath my wings.
It must have been cold there in my shadow
to never have sunlight on your face.
You were content to let me shine, that's your way.
You always walked a step behind.

It was the song, *"Wind Beneath My Wings"* (by Lee Greenwood). For all my past success, I had received the accolades while Patsy stayed quietly in the background. Yet, I never knew how much this song would extend like eagles wings into our marriage. I could never have succeeded in my career without her. Patsy was always the wind beneath my wings.

Later that evening, when Patsy opened the envelope I had given her, I saw her eyes fill with tears. She looked at me with such love... and then she smiled and began to laugh.

I stared at her, baffled, thinking, *"What's so funny? Did I miss something? Was the card too juvenile?"*

She was still laughing, and the anticipation was killing me. Patsy just reached into her handbag and handed me an envelope. My hands were shaking as I slowly opened it.

It was a card. On the front were a little boy and a little girl. They were sitting on a beach, looking out at the ocean with his arm wrapped shyly around her shoulders. On the outside it said, "You and me..." and inside it said, "...were meant to be." Patsy had the same feeling I did... like we were both little children again, falling in love for the first time.

"You and Me ... Were Meant to Be."

The two cards were so beautiful and fitting — different, but matching in such an unusual way. It was as if we were starting all over again. I took her hands and kissed them, and in that moment, all of our differences just melted away. Our hearts were filled with forgiveness for all the hurt and wrongs that we had inflicted on each other. Like God's divine forgiveness, ours was simply given, and our hearts were one.

How fitting that this would come on our anniversary! It took nineteen years for us to finally understand why we got married in the first place. It was because we loved each other, and now we were putting that first, with God's help.

Later we framed the cards and hung them on our wall for all our friends to see. We found out then that many of our friends had expected us to divorce, so they were glad to see that we had reconciled.

Patsy and I had reached an understanding without needing to discuss any of the issues that had plagued us over the years. The walls came down, and we both realized that we were so much in love with each other that nothing, absolutely nothing else mattered. Just as Jesus had calmed the sea for his apostles, he had calmed our marriage. Looking back on it now, I can see how all of this was necessary for God's plan.

Patsy and I decided right then that we needed to expand our family. So you must be thinking about the pitter-patter of little feet. But we were not like Abraham and Sarah who were blessed so late in life. Next, you might think that we were going to adopt. Well, kind-of, sort-of... but this adoption was going to have four paws. Patsy and I started to search for a Golden Retriever pup so we could become a mom and dad and start all over again.

CHAPTER 2

God's Protection

During the fall of 2005, things were getting hectic.
Patsy was working as the controller in the company
that Patsy and I had started. We had just lost an important
staff member, and Patsy was short on help. She was
responsible for all the books for a multimillion-dollar
wireless construction company. Patsy had always been
conscientious and hardworking. The late hours and heavy
workload were wearing her down.

Patsy had been subject to migraines ever since I had
known her. The pain could be so intense that she would
sometimes have to stay in bed for several days. This time it
was a vicious cycle. The stress of her workload made the
migraines more frequent and more severe, causing her to fall
further behind in her work. That, in turn, led to longer hours
and more migraines.

Patsy had always used a heavy dose of Goody Powder to stave off the pain, but this time it was not enough. She went online without my knowledge and purchased some Xanax of questionable quality. I had already warned Patsy how the excessive use of Goody Powder could cause internal bleeding. But as stubborn as she was, she ignored me and hid the fact that she was adding the Xanax to the mix.

Sometime later, I discovered what she had been taking. I was very upset with Patsy and even more so at her supplier. He found out how enraged I was when he called her one day, and I grabbed the phone and answered it. I warned him that I would send *Guido* to his house to take care of all "family business." I told him that if he ever called here again or gave her any more product, there would be a price to pay... a price he could not afford. I can assure you that he never called again. However, it may have been that toxic combination coupled with the extra workload that helped to weaken Patsy's immune system.

I was worried about Patsy and wanted to get her away from all that stress for a while. So, toward the end of December, we took two of our daughters and their families on a Disney Cruise. We had done the same thing two years earlier, but this cruise was very special for Patsy and me with our newfound love and understanding. It made for a more exciting cruise. It was a time to remember for all of us, having fun together and feeling the strong bonds of family. Patsy and I were having the time of our lives. When the ship came to port, Patsy and I were anxious to get home to pick up our new little bundle of joy.

Waiting for us at the Atlanta Airport would be the newest member of our family, Billy-the-Kid, a Golden Retriever pup. We were excited to finally meet Billy. We had bought him from a well-known breeder in California and had scheduled his arrival to coincide with our returning flight. He was already potty trained and had been through obedience training. The plus was that he was also trained as a service dog. Who knew that his services would be needed in the near future?

I will never forget the moment I met Billy. I had arrived at Delta's hub center. I walked into this big warehouse with all kinds of parcels being staged for pickup. That's when I saw Billy's kennel.

It was sitting all by itself in the huge complex, and a Delta attendant was giving Billy some water. I walked up to the kennel and looked through the slotted, metal door to see Billy's gentle demeanor and his beautiful face.

Even though he was just six months old, he didn't make a sound, but sat there as still as the waters of a lake on a clear, calm summer night. His tranquil demeanor captured me.

He looked at me, turned his head to the side as Goldens do, and gave me a look as if to say, "*Hey bud! Are you the guy that's going to get me out of here? I've only been flying for five hours?"*

I took Billy out of the kennel and walked him to the car where Patsy was waiting for me. She was bubbling over with delight when she saw Billy. You could see that Billy would have done well as a show dog. His behavior for a six-month-old was so mature that, if I hadn't known his age, I would have thought he was an adult. He reminded me of Airbud in the movie. In fact, Billy did come from around the Hollywood area, so he could have been one of Airbud's cousins.

Billy took to us immediately. When I picked him up to put him in the car, he parked himself comfortably in Patsy's lap for the ride as if he had done it a hundred times before, and off we sailed for home.

I was driving and just gazing at Billy, not really paying attention to the road. As I was about to merge onto I-75, I veered into the adjacent lane without noticing that there was a car next to me. I suddenly found that my left rear bumper was locked to the right front bumper of the other car. For a short time we were one vehicle, joined at the bumpers like Siamese twins. My heart started pounding, and my adrenaline kicked in. I was very tense, but extremely focused.

I knew I was in a very difficult situation, terrified that, with all the traffic, we could get ourselves into a deadly accident. I knew that, in order to get released, the other driver and I were going to have to work in perfect sync. I would have to brake slowly, and he would have to ease off the gas ever so gently and turn to the left, hoping no cars were next to him… all this at 60 mph. And we had to do this with no communication, not even hand signals. Could this guy read my mind to keep this bumper lock from turning into a total disaster?

I can tell you now that God was directing us both with the perfect timing only He could arrange. We did unlock bumpers, and there was a big sigh of relief from Patsy and me. Billy cocked his head as if to say, *"What just happened?"*

We both pulled off to the side of the road, and I slumped over the wheel for a moment to regain my composure. I couldn't believe that we were all sitting there without a scratch or a bruise. I had thought for sure we were doomed. I had no idea how we escaped, but I was thankful. Then I took a deep breath and got out of the car.

When I saw the guy coming toward me, I couldn't believe my eyes. It was an Atlanta police officer. I looked at his car and saw that it was not a police car. It was his own personal car!

As we walked toward each other, I really expected him *to start yelling at me or maybe put the cuffs on me.* I knew it was my fault. I felt stupid and ashamed of my stupidity.

"I'm so sorry, officer," I began as I extended my hand, thinking he could cuff me right then. I knew that my carelessness could have gotten us all killed, and we had narrowly escaped a major pile-up.

To my surprise, he didn't yell or cuff me. He shook my hand and just looked relieved. "Yeah, that was a close one. Glad you knew what to do."

"I didn't know what to do," I replied, "but God did."

"Amen to that," he said.

Then he looked at his bumper and shrugged. "Looks like this old beater just took another beating."

"I can't tell you how sorry I am..." I began again, but he cut me off.

"Don't worry about it. The bumper was already bent. I just use this heap to get back and forth to work. I've got to get home for a date night with my wife, and I'm running late. If I'm late... well, you know how it is."

I couldn't believe what I was hearing. This had never happened to me before, receiving a "GET OUT OF JAIL FREE" card. I thought that only happened in the game of Monopoly. And we narrowly escaped a major pile-up. I thought that only happened in action-packed car-chase movies.

I said to him, "At least let me pay for the damages."

"Nah, that's okay," he said, glancing over at Patsy and Billy. "It looks like you've got someone waiting for you, too." Billy had his head out the window and his tongue hanging out. Both of them must have been hoping and praying that I wasn't going to jail. My heart was filled with love and gratitude

I couldn't leave it like that. I had damaged his car, and I wanted to make restitution. I took $300 out of my wallet and handed it to the man.

"No, that's okay," he said.

"Please, sir, take this," I replied. "If nothing else, take your wife out somewhere special."

At that, he grinned, took the money, and shook my hand. "Thank you and God bless... oh, by the way, drive carefully."

I stood there dumbfounded as he walked to his car and drove off.

God was watching over Patsy and me that night. His timing was perfect. He knew what was to happen in the weeks to come, and I believe He didn't want anything to interfere with the miracle He was about to bestow on us.

I believe that everything happens for a reason, but sometimes we don't see the reason until we look back and reflect on how events of the past lead into the events of the future. At the time I didn't know why it had turned out that way. I just thanked God for keeping us safe.

I also believe that nobody leaves this earth with unfinished work for God... *nobody!*

CHAPTER 3

The Inevitable Was About to Happen.

T hey say that hindsight is 20/20. As I look back now, I can pick out warning signs along the way that I completely missed at the time. The event that stands out most clearly in my mind occurred in December of 2003. It was our first Disney cruise, and our entire family was going.

We had arrived at Cape Canaveral, where the Disney ship was waiting. We were waiting in the cruise line's main center, ready to board the ship, when Patsy suddenly became disoriented. She just stood there... completely oblivious to her surroundings with the strangest look on her face. I started to talk to her, but all she did was to stare out into the abyss. I couldn't get her to recognize me let alone talk to me.

And the look on her face was almost diabolical! A wave of fear swept over me. The episode lasted only a short time, but it felt much longer.

I thought about not boarding and taking Patsy to a hospital. However, we had the doctor of the cruise line check her out, and Patsy had returned to her normal self with no symptoms at all. The doctor thought she might have had a bad reaction to some medicine she had taken. In my gut, I knew it was more than a reaction to medicine.

Patsy, being the trooper she is — and oh, by the way, stubborn as a mule — wanted to carry on and board the ship. I wasn't sure if that was the right decision, but when Patsy sets her mind to something, you would have a better chance of convincing a starving lion not to eat you than of changing Patsy's mind.

I was still reluctant to board the ship, knowing this could happen again, but we did, and we did have a great family get-to-together. Patsy didn't have any more episodes while on the cruise or afterward, and the incident was temporarily forgotten. It would be two more years before this beast would show its ugly head again.

Back from the cruise in late December of 2005, Patsy seemed to be more relaxed, and she hadn't had a migraine for a while. Even though the work had piled up in her absence, she seemed to be handling it well. I was scheduled for my twice-yearly visit to Duke University's Diet and

Fitness Center on January 8. I had been attending their program in North Carolina for about three years.

As I always explained it, "You know, when you start to become middle-aged, the battle of the bulge begins."

I would like everybody to think that was the truth of the matter, but it wasn't. I had fought a weight problem from my teenage years on, and it was beginning to affect my health in other ways.

When I was in Atlanta, I often wore basketball shorts with the Duke insignia, and people would ask me if I went to Duke.

I would say, "Yes, as a matter of fact, I do." If they didn't ask any more questions, I wouldn't volunteer any more information.

If they asked what I studied, I would say, "I'm studying how to keep the fat off."

Then they'd ask me if I was studying to be a dietician, and I would reply, "Something like that, but I'm my only client." That got either a big laugh or a puzzled look.

Anyhow, I was off to Duke. I packed up my bike, my dog, and my personal belongings and headed into the sunset with no hint of what I was to face in a few short weeks.

The next week was a typical, uneventful time – eating right, exercising, socializing with all the friends I had made there, and working on and learning about health and fitness.

Ron, Hank Aaron, and Another Friend at
Duke Diet & Fitness Center

It was also a time for bonding with our new pup, Billy. He loved to retrieve tennis balls and Frisbees. I even threw a license plate, and he retrieved that. There was nothing he wouldn't retrieve — even a rock. When I would ride my bike, Billy would run right beside me for miles. I was having fun. It was a good week.

Billy-the-Kid

It was now Saturday, January 14. I had just gotten back to my room after a long bike ride with Billy when the phone rang. It was my son-in-law, Jimmy. I could tell by his voice that something was wrong.

Patsy had been visiting our daughter Amy and granddaughter Savanah in Chattanooga where Savanah was competing in a cheerleading competition. Jimmy said that Amy had found Patsy putting eye makeup on her cheek and that Patsy was continuing to act strangely.

It took a moment for me to grasp. I became very tense and concerned. "Okay, Jimmy," I said. "I'm flying home on the first plane out, and I am taking Patsy back to Duke tonight. I am going to get her checked out. You drive Patsy back to Atlanta, and pick me up at the airport."

I thanked Jimmy and hung up. I immediately grabbed Billy, and left for the airport. I didn't even wait to make a reservation. I just went. When I arrived at the airport, there was a flight that was leaving soon. However, Billy could not fly without clearance from a vet because of the cold weather – a regulation *I had never heard of before*!

It was early afternoon on Saturday. The only way I could reach my vet was at her office, and I knew she closed at one p.m. on Saturdays.

"Please, God, make the vet be there," I prayed.

You know when you ask, you will get an answer although it may not always be the one you want. In this case, the answer was, "Hello, this is Dr. Chan."

I couldn't believe it. She was there. She'd had an emergency patient that day which had carried her past the regular closing time. She faxed over Billy's clearance, and we flew home. I couldn't thank God enough. Billy could never have flown home without that clearance.

My son-in-law had dropped Patsy off at the house and picked me up at the airport. As we were driving home, I asked Jimmy about Patsy's episode of putting eyeliner on her cheek.

Jimmy didn't really know a lot more about the incident. He said, "I told Patsy that you were coming back to take her to Duke to get her checked out. And she had a cow!"

"What do you mean?" I asked.

She said, 'NO WAY!' "Then she told me she just wanted to go home, and she wasn't going to Duke. She didn't need to go to Duke. She just needed to go home and get some rest."

"I asked him, "Did you ask her if she wanted to come to the airport?"

"I did," he answered. "I thought she would be excited to see you, but she said that she was just tired and wanted to stay home. I tried to convince her to come, but no luck."

"Well, I appreciate you trying, but, you know when Patsy makes up her mind, it's cast in stone. I knew I had my work cut out for me convincing Patsy to come back to Duke to get checked out. But I was determined I would not lose this battle.

When I arrived home and walked into the house, Patsy was standing by the door. I think she had been watching for me. I knew I had to put on my tough-guy act. I looked at her, trying to think of what to say, and all I could come up with was, "Enough is enough!"

She just looked at me, surprised. "Something is seriously wrong with you," I said. "You need to come back with me to Duke and get a complete checkup."

I could sense her stubbornness rising as she said, "I can't, Ron! I'm way behind in my work at the office. I'm okay!"

That's my Patsy! She had just been told that there was something seriously wrong with her, and all she was worried about was how much work she had to do.

"Patsy," I said, "the work can wait. Your health is more important."

"No, Ron," she said, beginning to back away. "I'm just going to lie down for a little while, and then I'll be fine." She turned and started for the bedroom.

"NO, PATSY!" I said, my voice rising along with my frustration. "The way I see it, you have two options. You can pack your clothes, and we can leave for Duke, or I can pack your clothes and tie you up, and then we can leave for Duke. Either way, you are coming with me NOW!"

"You can't make me go!" she said defiantly. "I'm fine, and I'm staying right here. You go back and finish your session there."

I was feeling inept at my inability to get through to her. "Patsy, I'll do what I have to do!"

Jimmy sensed the intensity of the argument and bravely intervened. He said "Patsy, you need to go with Ron. This could be very serious."

Jimmy's words made me realize that my hard-nosed approach wasn't working... I needed to revise my strategy. So, I got down on my knees, and begged her. And I do mean begged her!

Patsy could see the tears in my eyes, and she started to soften, realizing how much I cared. Perhaps, too, she had begun to realize that something actually might be wrong. How better to check it out than at one of best hospitals in the world?

I thanked Jimmy, Patsy packed, we grabbed Billy, and we were off to the airport that same night. At this point, Billy was racking up some serious frequent flyer miles. Remember that just a few weeks ago he had flown from California to join our family. He was already picking out his next vacation spot with the mileage he was earning.

We arrived in Durham late that night and went right to bed. The next day was Sunday, so we just relaxed and enjoyed each other's company. There were no further signs that anything was wrong with Patsy. On Monday, January

16, I enrolled Patsy in a very comprehensive testing program — from the top of her head to the bottoms of her feet.

Patsy underwent all kinds of testing, EKG, EEG, and a complete cat scan of her whole body, including her brain. She had blood work, urinalysis, a stress test, lung x-rays, head x-rays, and others I can't even remember. It was a complete week of testing from Monday morning to Friday afternoon.

All the doctors that tested her, including the infection specialist, found nothing wrong... absolutely nothing! They were all perplexed. The virus hid from all those tests the way a viper snake hides behind a rock or in a hole, ready to strike its prey. It was just a question of when it would show itself.

It was now Friday afternoon, and I was filled with anxiety. I knew something was wrong with Patsy. I had been certain that Duke Hospital would find the cause, but they found nothing. None of this made sense, and I didn't know what to do. Furthermore, Patsy was highly stressed from all the testing and she needed some way to get rid of the tension. I thought that a massage would help her relax. Patsy agreed, and she took advantage of the hotel service.

That night, we went to dinner with a bunch of my friends with whom I had built a relationship over the few years I had been attending Duke. Patsy was unusually quiet during dinner. I knew she was tired, and she tends to be shy in a group. However, I was very concerned about her well-being, and that played on my mind all through dinner.

Looking back, I could see that she was not just quiet, but quiet to the point of being unresponsive. It may have been the massage that roused the monster from its sleep. Without any warning, the beast was about to strike again.

CHAPTER 4

A Time of Darkness

The next morning was January 22. I woke up with my heart still heavy, not knowing what was wrong with Patsy. I decided it would be a good idea to take her to breakfast. I rolled over and tapped her on the shoulder. "Would you like to go and get some breakfast?"

"No thanks," she murmured, "I'm not feeling too well. I just want to sleep a little bit more." I had hoped that a good night's rest would have made her feel better, but her words were disheartening.

I felt her forehead. She was warm as if she might have a slight temperature. "Okay," I said, trying to sound cheerful. "You just rest. I'll go get breakfast."

I went out and brought back her favorite breakfast, coffee, and a cheese Danish pastry. When I walked into the hotel room, Patsy was standing in the middle of the room staring into space. Her demeanor and the look on her face were like something out of a scene from *The Walking Dead*. Shocked, I dropped the coffee and cheese Danish on the floor and stared at her.

"Patsy! What's *wrong*?" I asked in a highly emotional voice.

There was no response – no sign that she had heard me or that she was even aware of my presence. That grim-reaper look was like nothing I had ever seen in my life... except once before. In that instant, I was transported back two years to the Disney cruise center, waiting to board the ship, but even that could not compare to what I was experiencing now. I felt the same wave of fear, but much more intensely, and I struggled to fight the panic rising from the pit of my stomach.

"Please, God. Help!" I cried. I tried yelling, "Patsy! Patsy!"... to see if I could break through her state of oblivion. But she gave no sign of coherency. It was as if she had perished, but yet she was still standing. I grabbed her arms and shook her to wake her. No response.

"Oh, no! Dear God!" I cried out! The beast had arrived like a thief in the night and stolen the vibrancy and the life right out of my Patsy.

"Patsy, Patsy... what have you done to yourself?" I hugged her tightly, tears rolling down my face. "It's that Xanax... the Goody Powder... You've poisoned yourself! Why wouldn't you listen to me?! You never, ever listen!"

Although I knew the situation was serious, I had no idea that this was just the tip of the iceberg. At that moment, I was simply driven by panic and filled with fear and anxiety that were almost paralyzing. The fight-or-flight mode kicked in, and I chose both. I scooped Patsy up and fled to the car, fighting for breath. The struggle to get her into the car in her unresponsive state left me gasping. I stuck to my resolve and finally managed to get us both into the car and underway, racing at top speed for Duke Hospital.

It was only five minutes away, but, for me, time just stopped. In a dreamlike state, I was driving in slow motion through a time warp filled with my churning emotions. All the while, I was hoping and praying and crying. I was pleading and begging God repeatedly to *make everything be okay.*

When we arrived at the emergency entrance, I jumped out of the car, rushed around to the passenger's side, and picked Patsy up. I dashed into the emergency room yelling at the top of my lungs, "*My wife... my wife is sick! Help me! Please help me!!*"

I was immediately surrounded by staff who quickly took her into a room while I was crying my heart out. "Please,

Patsy. Please, Patsy, be okay!" I sobbed. "Oh God! Oh God! Help her! Please, God, help her!" I was an emotional train wreck.

A nurse was trying to talk to me. She needed information about Patsy, and I knew I had to get myself under control. I mustered all my willpower and finally settled down enough to control my labored breathing. I could finally speak well enough to tell the nurse about all the testing she had undergone at Duke in the last week. I also told her about the incident where Patsy put eye makeup on her cheek and about the brief episode that had occurred two years earlier before the cruise.

Patsy's fever was a little over 106 degrees. They wanted me to wait outside in the waiting room. But I refused.

"No way!" I said. "I'm not leaving my wife. I'm staying right here with her." And there I stayed... and thank God I did.

After briefly examining Patsy, they told me that she had either a viral or bacterial infection or possibly meningitis. They needed to do a spinal tap to figure out what was going on. They left us alone and went to find a doctor who could perform the procedure.

They had already given her Tylenol in an IV with fluids, but Patsy was still burning up. It was taking a while, and I was consumed with worry. I knew it was critical to get her fever down quickly to prevent brain damage. I went to the nurse's station and said, "My wife is burning up with fever. Can you get someone *now* to get her temperature down?"

I couldn't believe what the nurse said to me then. "You are overreacting. We are working on it. Just go back to her room and wait."

"*Wait?*" I unloaded on her. "*I am not overreacting! If this was someone you loved, you would not just sit around and wait for her brain to burn up! Get someone here NOW!*"

By the time I returned to her room, they were already bringing ice packs to cool her down and lower her temperature more quickly. Patsy was in and out of consciousness.

Finally, a doctor came to perform the spinal tap. He was very young. In fact, he looked like he was straight out of high school. He did not project a warm, fuzzy feeling. He started the procedure, but he was having a difficult time getting the needle in the right spot, and he seemed awfully unsure of himself.

I was frantic. "*Enough!*" I shouted. "*Go get an experienced doctor! I want someone who knows how to do this procedure... right NOW!*" The poor guy scurried out of the room, his ego and confidence wounded, no doubt, by my ill temper.

I didn't realize at the time that this illness was so rare that there was no set protocol for handling it, and the resulting chaos fueled my anger. In retrospect and in fairness to the staff, I realize that none of them had a clue what they were dealing with, how serious it was, or what to do about it. But to me, at the time, they just seemed inept. My anger and determination became the leading force in creating and maintaining the necessary sense of urgency.

When the new doctor arrived, I assisted in keeping Patsy still. He completed the procedure in minutes without incident. Then he told me that it would take three days to grow a culture to find out what kind of bacteria or virus Patsy had contracted. In the meantime, they would start her on an anti-bacterial, anti-viral cocktail to lower the fever and, if we were lucky, knock out some of the infection. But he would still not know exactly how to treat it until the culture came back... in three days.

They finally brought Patsy's fever down, but only to about 101. At least, she was stable and able to start talking to me again although she was frequently confused. And she was scared. I was relieved that they were admitting her, but I was very concerned about leaving her alone in her condition, especially not knowing what to expect.

I called my sister Bernadette who lived in Cleveland. "Bernie," I said. "I need your help. Patsy is extremely sick, and no one knows what it is. I don't know what's going to happen, but I am very concerned. I need you to come."

"When?"

"Right now!"

She must have heard the desperation in my voice. My sister has a loving heart, and she said, "I'll start packing."

"Thanks, Bernie." I told her how much I loved her and then said, "I'll book you on the first flight to Raleigh and call you back with the details."

Bernie had a full-time job at a law firm in Cleveland and was part of the administrative team. I didn't know then, but she called her boss and told him she would have to leave for an indefinite amount of time.

Her boss, Bill Rini, was gracious enough to say, "Bernie, don't worry. We have you covered." God was using His angels to provide protection for Patsy.

By 5 p.m., my sister was in Raleigh. When she arrived at the hospital, she immediately found her way to Patsy's room. Seeing her in the doorway, I felt a weight lift from my shoulders.

Patsy's dinner was just being served. Earlier in the day, she had been able to feed herself lunch with only a little help from me, but dinner was another story. She was beginning to decline, and I had to feed her like a two-year-old child.

As I was feeding Patsy, I turned my head and saw the look on my sister's face — a look of dismay and complete disbelief. My heart sank, but I knew I could count on Bernie to watch over my precious Patsy.

Bernie was truly God sent. I have severe sleep apnea and cannot sleep without a machine. I was emotionally drained but relieved that Patsy wouldn't be left alone. I could be there for Patsy in the morning. Bernie would stay the night and look after Patsy. Even though Duke is an excellent hospital, nurses have multiple patients to care for, and things have a way of slipping through the cracks. And, sure enough, they would here as well.

It was about 1 a.m. that night as I was getting ready to leave when Patsy struggled out of bed and grabbed hold of me, not wanting me to leave... like a child not wanting her parents to go out and leave her with a babysitter. It was so hard for me to leave, but I knew I needed rest so that I could take over for my sister tomorrow. My heart was hurting as it had never hurt before. If my heart could have cried, it would have.

I stayed a little longer and then had to go through it all over again, with Patsy clinging to me, not wanting me to leave. Her illness was gradually devouring her, and it hadn't even fully kicked in yet. I left with such sadness; my heart wanted to bleed tears.

When I arrived at the hotel room, I couldn't sleep. The worry was unbearable. I felt like I wanted to die. I wanted to escape from the mental and emotional torture. Around 4 a.m., my hotel room phone rang. Each time it rang it struck me like the sound of someone flipping the switch on the electric chair... like the ending to all thought and feeling and pain. But I was still alive, and each ring struck me harder and harder until the pain was unbearable.

I could not answer it. I started bawling... "*She is dead! She is dead!*" I couldn't stop crying. "*Please, God, save her! Please, God, save her, God,*" I begged.

I just lay there, not wanting to face the news from the other end of the line. After a while, I got up and took a shower, crying the whole time. I could hardly dress, but I finally got some clothes on. Then I went slowly back to the hospital. Entering in a daze, I felt my world just stand still. I couldn't understand why the rest of the world was still moving on.

When I reached Patsy's room, she was not there, and neither was my sister. My heart stopped. I knew my worst fears had become reality. I started crying hard. I could barely make it to the nurses' station.

"What's wrong?" asked the nurse behind the desk. "What happened?"

I could not speak. I could not stop crying. The nurse called for help. I was immediately surrounded by hospital staff, but I was so incoherent that they didn't know what was wrong with me. They began trying to comfort me and were also trying to find out what was going on.

Finally, after many attempts to speak, I managed to ask, "Where is my wife?"

"Who is your wife?" asked one of the staff.

I couldn't get the words out. I was hyperventilating. Finally, I managed to choke out, "Patsy... Patsy Tripodo."

"Oh, Patsy Tripodo... yes, Patsy was taken upstairs to the ICU."

"She's alive?" I asked, my voice trembling.

"Yes, she's alive. She's in a coma. They helped induce the coma to try to stabilize her vital signs."

I jumped up and ran up the two flights of steps. Following me were two of the staff members who were very concerned. As I approached the ICU, I found that I was blocked by a locked door which was controlled from inside by a buzzer.

I tried to speak to the voice box, but all I could do was babble. Eventually, the staff members who had followed me caught up. They showed me to a chair and waited for me to calm down. I knew I had to regain my composure so that I could make rational decisions about Patsy's care. I struggled to slow my breathing down. By focusing on my breathing I was gradually able to regain control.

A nurse came out of the locked ICU doors to explain what was being done for Patsy. She told me that the machines Patsy was hooked up to were state-of-the-art. A nurse would be by Patsy's side every minute, monitoring the settings on the machine to maximize the benefits while watching for negative responses. She tried to paint a picture of what I would see when I entered Patsy's room, but I was still so engulfed by emotion that I could barely follow what she was saying. Then, she walked me through the locked door and down the hall to Patsy's room.

The door was closed, and I opened it slowly. There was no way that someone could have prepared me for what I was about to see! There were massive, futuristic-looking machines hovering all around Patsy with their tentacles hooked to her body. It looked like a scene out of *Star Wars*. As I glanced around the room, I could see that Patsy was also on a life-support ventilator with a nurse standing by.

I closed my eyes and just stood there. I was devastated.

Random thoughts flashed through my mind. For a moment, I was back in Cleveland, Ohio, where I had spent my early years, praying to God in my old church. It was there in that childhood environment that my perception of God was formed. After I moved to Georgia, I encountered people whose perspectives were very different, and I began to rethink my own faith. One of the things I kept hearing in Georgia was: *When you ask for a miracle, expect it.*

"Well, let me try that," I thought. *"Maybe that will work, and God will heal Patsy."* I had no idea how to negotiate a miracle with God, but I was going to try. I wanted to believe I could do it, and I would try very hard to believe I could do it. I thought if I kept saying it over and over again, maybe I would believe it enough that I could actually do it. But I did have very serious doubts.

As I proceeded into the room, I was shaken. Patsy was as white as a ghost. l wanted to hold her in my arms, but the machines would not allow that. I squeezed in between two machines so I could get close enough to touch her. Silently I cried out to God, *"Please, please, heal her, Lord."*

I wanted to believe, but the way she looked, hooked to all those machines, made it very difficult to believe that even God could save her. But I had to try. I had to see if expecting a miracle could produce a miracle.

That was the first time I said it... in the room with my sister and just one nurse attending the machines. *"Jesus is going to heal my wife!"*

My sister said, "Ronnie, I hope so."

I thought to myself, "*Me too.*" Then I hugged Bernie. She could feel the pain in my heart, and it was killing her too.

A short time later, one of the doctors came in and told me that they were treating the fever by pumping the blood out of her body, cooling it, and then pumping it back in. It would be two more days before the results of the culture would come back to identify the type of brain infection she had. He said that her chances of surviving at all were less than 10 percent. If she did live, she would probably have both severe motor and mental impairment and would likely be completely bedridden.

That was the second time I said it. "*Jesus is going to heal her, doctor.*" And I said it with the biggest knot in my stomach. I wanted to throw up right then. As I look back, I can only imagine what the doctor must have thought, seeing my total distress.

The pain was so severe that I could hardly function. For the rest of the day and into the night, I kept a vigil over Patsy with Bernie at my side. That's when my sister told me what had happened the previous night.

Patsy had started going into a coma, and Bernie could sense that something wasn't right. Like me, my sister is very persistent, and she kept telling the night nurse that something was wrong. The nurse said that my wife was just sleeping deeply, but Bernie could tell that Patsy wasn't just sleeping. Her body looked lifeless. Finally, Bernie went to the nurses' station and demanded that another nurse come and look at Patsy.

The second nurse took one look at Patsy and recognized right away that she was going into a coma. The nurse sounded an alarm and the staff immediately started swarming the room. They took Patsy up to the ICU unit where they started the process of hooking her up to the life support *Star Wars* machine. Thank God my sister was there. God had every base covered.

From then on, I began telling everyone that Jesus was going to heal my wife. But, no matter how confident I appeared on the outside, on the inside I was being eaten alive by worry and doubt... doubt that God was really listening to my prayers.

"Who am I?" I thought. *"God's not going to hear my prayers. Maybe Billy Graham's, but surely not mine."*

I also had selfish worries about what kind of life I would have if my wife were an invalid. What a hypocrite I was, letting everybody think that I was this man of strong faith who had God's ear, telling people that God was going to heal his wife! What I needed and didn't have was the grace that only God can give you to have faith and trust in Him. Back then, I had no understanding of what grace is or what grace can do. But I was going to find out.

CHAPTER 5

If You Ask for a Miracle, Expect It.

T he days ahead were a waiting game. I was tormented by another problem, one of my own making. It concerned Patsy's daughter Amy. She needed to know what had happened to her mom. Patsy and Amy shared a strong bond of love, and I knew I had to call Amy, but I couldn't do it. I kept putting it off because I knew that Amy would be devastated by her mom's illness, and I was afraid she would not be strong enough to handle it. Truthfully, I was really afraid I would not be strong enough to handle her emotional state along with my own.

Finally, I called her husband, Jimmy, the one who had brought Patsy back to Atlanta after the eye makeup incident. We had always been close.

"Jimmy, I don't have the heart to tell Amy. You'll have to tell her."

"Tell her what?"

"Her mom is in intensive care. She's hooked up to some kind of life support with an illness that is so rare nobody has figured it out yet."

There was a pause. Then, "What did you say?"

"Sit down, Jimmy." I waited a moment. Then I said, "Just get Amy here quickly. Tell her that her mom is very sick and needs her, and that's all you know. The less you tell her, the better for now."

Amy had a tendency to become overly anxious back then. As much as she loved her mom, I was afraid the full story at one time could be terribly upsetting. Better to let it come in small doses. If Amy needed emotional support, she would have her family and friends around her as well as medical help if needed.

After I hung up, I started calling the troops — all the people I knew who were prayer warriors. To all of them, I said, "God is going to heal Patsy, but she needs your prayers." People started coming from all over Atlanta, Florida, and other nearby areas to pray for Patsy.

One good friend, Rev. Lawrence Reeves, pastor of an Atlanta church, visited Patsy and me at the hospital. He had known Patsy as a lovely, vibrant woman, but after he took one look at her, he didn't say anything for a moment.

"God's going to heal her, Reverend," I said.

"You're right, Ron. Amen to that," he replied, as if he had trouble mustering up the words.

Years later, he told me that Patsy had looked so awful, all bulked up from the fluids they were giving her intravenously, that he didn't even recognize her. He was shocked and saddened. He could not imagine any way that Patsy could recover from the condition she was in. And, I can tell you, without Jesus, she wouldn't have.

On the third day, we received the test results. Two doctors brought me into a room, sat me down, and proceeded to tell me what Patsy had contracted. They told me it was a very rare virus with fewer than two thousand cases a year. The beast's name was herpes simplex encephalitis (HSE).

The doctors compared it to shingles, a result of the chicken pox virus, which can hide inside your nerve cells for years until your immune system is compromised. Then it re-emerges as shingles, usually in the form of painful lesions on the surface of your skin, but it can also travel through the spinal cord, attack your brain, and destroy it bit by bit.

The HSE virus had done the same thing to Patsy. There are different severities of this illness. The doctors told me that Patsy had it full blown. On a scale from 1 to 10 —10 meaning that you die — Patsy was an 8 or a 9. They said her chances of surviving were less than 10 percent. And, if she did live, she would be seriously impaired and her life would hardly be worth living. So, in essence, they were telling me... she had no chance.

I started to cry profusely. It took a few minutes to pull myself together, and in that time the words came back to me — *If you ask for a miracle, expect it.*

I wiped my eyes, looked up, and said, "Jesus is going to heal my wife."

I don't know why I even said it. I'd just been crying my eyes out in despair. But I wanted to believe that Jesus was going to heal Patsy. My inconsistency could scarcely lend credibility to my words. My thoughts and emotions were ricocheting all over the place. I'm sure they thought that I was going to end up in the hospital as well.

People continued coming to see Patsy. Amy finally arrived. I was not sure what to expect. I kept saying to Amy as well as everyone else that Jesus was going to heal her, hiding my fear and worry as best I could. Amy, to my relief, handled the situation better than I had expected... in fact, better than I had been doing. The problem I had been anticipating never even occurred.

I had been putting it off, but I knew I had to go back to Atlanta. I had neglected my duties as president and CEO, and I had to get people paid and put my affairs in order. The company was in a holding pattern as well. But all my employees had stepped up their game to compensate for the void Patsy and I had left in the company. I had a heavy weight on my back, not realizing that God was carrying most of the load. I flew home for a couple of days, caught up on some of my work, and delegated some of my authority to key people in the company so I could return to Patsy.

I was on my way to the Atlanta airport to catch a flight back to Raleigh when I received a call from Henry, the broker who was negotiating the listing of my business. The buyer and I hadn't been able to come to terms on the price or how much I would hold as a note.

I answered the phone. "How are you, Henry?"

"Great, Ron. You are not going to believe this. The guy that wants to buy your company has offered you your full asking price plus all the money up front at closing!"

As I look back, I can see that God was already offering a way out of the business so I could work directly for Him. But

I didn't get it. The offer didn't even excite me as it should have. I had really wanted to sell the company, but, at that moment, I was so distraught that I couldn't even think about it.

I said, "I've changed my mind and don't want to sell right now."

"Have you lost your mind?" Henry asked. "This is the deal of a lifetime!"

"Henry, I'm sorry, I have too much going on. I just need some space. Patsy is my only concerned."

I have no idea why I said that. It was an incredible deal, the kind you dream about. Normally, I would have jumped at the opportunity. But, if I had, the course of my life would have changed drastically, and I might never have written this book.

I flew back to Raleigh where I was to meet Dave, one of my lifelong friends from the third grade who had come to be by my side. By the time I landed, he was already waiting by the curb at arrivals. I walked outside to his car and began opening the door. The door was partway open when I heard a clear, distinctive, echoing voice.

It said, "**Ron, this is not about you. This is about Me. And your wife will be healed**."

"What?" I said. "Dave, what did you say?" I opened the door wide.

Dave shook his head. "I didn't say anything,"

"Wait a minute, Dave. I heard you... you said something," I insisted.

A bit annoyed, he said, "Just get in the car, Ronnie, and let's go. I did not say anything. Not one word."

I had never ever heard a voice like that before. The voice was so clear, so unique, and so majestic. It had to be God. Oh, there had been times when I thought I had heard God's voice, but the words were always prompted by my own thoughts. I had no thoughts that day as I was opening the car door... none. I believe that God wanted to make sure He had my full attention, to know that it was truly Him and not just my own thoughts. The more I thought about it, the more convinced I was that God had just spoken to me.

The voice gave me strength like I'd never had before. I knew now how Samson felt in the Bible. His voice was like a shot of adrenaline on steroids. My faith was suddenly stronger. I felt God's presence right beside me, and I had nothing to worry about. I believed that everything was going to be okay. I had begun, through Gods words, to feel the power of His grace.

I didn't want to say anything to Dave right then, but I couldn't hold my tongue. I said, "Dave, what I heard... it was God. God just spoke to me, and He told me Patsy was going to be healed."

Dave, being the jokester he is, asked, "Did He tell you the numbers for the lottery tonight?"

I'm sure Dave didn't know what to think at the time. Nevertheless, he drove me straight to the hospital. When I arrived at the ICU floor, my family and friends were already there, keeping a vigil and praying that Patsy would pull through. I could see Patsy's doctor from a distance through a door that was partly glass.

Patsy's sister, Peggy, was standing there looking very distraught. She said, "The doctor wants to see you."

I now had the grace of God's words which gave me the courage of a lion. I started to realize then what it means to put on the full armor of God. I looked at Peggy. "No matter what this doctor says, remember that he is just a man. I am telling you that Jesus is going to heal... and I mean fully heal... your sister." I will never forget the huge tears of hope running down Peggy's face. I hugged her and then started toward the door.

I proceeded through the door and down the hallway to meet the doctor. As I got close to him, I looked squarely into his eyes, and, with the authority of my God, I said: "Doc, Patsy is going to be healed."

The doctor looked at me, probably thinking either, *"You're completely nuts,"* or *"I hope you're right."* He simply nodded but did not comment on what I had said. Instead, he went straight into what he had to tell me.

"We believe that there is excessive pressure inside Patsy's head, and we need to monitor it. The only way to accurately monitor it is to drill a hole in the top of your wife's head close to her forehead. It is critical that we do this immediately to avoid further damage, and I need your permission."

"I'll give you my permission if you will pray with me," I answered.

The doctor was Jewish, but he readily agreed. After all, we pray to the same God. We held hands and I prayed out loud, even using Jesus' name. I felt a deeper peace with this prayer than I had ever felt before. When the prayer ended, the doctor squeezed my hand. Then he left to perform his job with the grace of God.

Hours passed before the doctor finally came out. "Mr. Tripodo, he said, "I can't believe it, but the pressure is stabilizing. However, she is not out of the woods by any means, and, if she pulls through, the prognosis for her quality of life is no better than it was two hours ago."

"Thank you, doctor," I said. "God has this handled."

I shook his hand and thanked him again. Then I walked away, knowing my God was with me. Silently, I was saying over and over again, *"Praise You, Jesus."*

For the next several days it was a waiting game again. I would spend hours in Patsy's room, but, with my ADHD, I had to move around a lot. I think the ADHD was amplified by the emotional upheaval I had experienced. It was hard to sit very long.

I walked down to the first floor, then back up, grabbing a cup of coffee. I would visit with people who came to see Patsy. I was on the phone a lot, managing my company from afar, taking and returning calls, and praying with family and friends. Working and being on the phone with family and friends was good because it kept my mind on other things. I could feel the love that people were sending. It was God's blessing, using other people to give me the comfort and support I needed.

When they were gone, I spent my time praying and reading the Bible. With my ADHD, I had never learned to read well, and I struggled immensely to understand the true meaning of God's words. A lot of the time, I got the gist of it, and it gave me comfort that His presence was there with me, but I longed to be able to read His word with total comprehension.

It brought me back to my grade school days. I had to battle with ADHD without even knowing that I had it. I was struggling to sit still and to focus long enough to learn basic reading skills. As I would find out later that was the key to learning everything else. Needless to say, I was far behind my classmates. I was in the sixth grade, and I didn't understand why I couldn't comprehend my schoolwork or retain the little bit that I did understand. I remember thinking about all the smart kids in my class who were receiving straight A's while I was receiving notes to my parents on how poorly I was doing.

I went to a parochial school where the teachers were tough on scholastics and discipline. I was so overwhelmed by my learning disability, that I would just check any box on the multiple choice tests hoping I would get lucky and, by chance, get some of the answers right—at least enough to make a passing grade. I did this a lot, and sometimes I would get a passing grade, but most of the time I wouldn't.

On one particular test in the sixth grade, I just checked off all the questions at random. The next day, my teacher told me to see her after class. I was sweating bullets, not knowing why I was in trouble. After class, I went to her desk, and she pulled out the test that I had played Russian roulette on.

She said to me, "did you study for this test?"

"Yes, Mrs. Mc Hugh," I said, lying through my teeth because I didn't have any idea how to study.

"I don't believe you did," she said. "You did not get a single answer right. In fact, some of your answers contradicted some of your other answers. That makes it clear you just checked any old box."

I thought to myself, "*My luck just ran out... I guess I should have eaten my Lucky Charms for breakfast yesterday!*"

"I did study," I said, trying to look sincere, "but maybe not long enough."

"LONG ENOUGH!" she exclaimed. "According to this test, you didn't even glance at the material! You take this note home, and I will see you and your mother on this matter," she said, as she handed me a sealed envelope.

That afternoon, going home, I was so scared of what was in the note that I thought about falling down in the mud so that it would cover the note and make it impossible to read. I knew I was in big trouble.

When I got home, my mom asked me if I'd had a good day at school. I thought to myself, "*Well, it was a good day until I got the note from my teacher. Now, I would call it a day I will never forget."*

I said to my mom, "Mrs. Mc Hugh gave me a note to give you."

"Oh, RONNIE!" she exclaimed smiling. "I hope this is a good report telling how much better you are doing."

"I have no idea, mom," I said, knowing full well it was not going to be a good report. But I was hoping for a miracle. "She just gave me the note after school and told me to give it to you when I get home."

When my mom opened the note and read it, she started to cry. I'm thinking, *"Why is she is crying? It must be worse than I thought. Oh boy, I'm in big trouble."*

Finally, she said, "Your teacher thinks you need to go to another school." She didn't want to tell me that it was a school for low IQ students. "Your teacher is suggesting the Julia Billiard School."

I knew what that meant. I said, "Mom, I don't want to go to *that* school. It's for dummies!"

My mom said, "I'm going to talk to your father first."

"Oh, no," I was thinking. *"Now I'm really in deep trouble."*

As it turned out, my father was in total agreement with my mom. The next day, my mom went to school with me and told my teacher that she was going to work even harder with my studies to get my grades up. Furthermore, she did not feel that her son needed *that* kind of school.

I was so relieved that I would not have to go to that school. If it wasn't for my mom, I don't think I would have made it past the sixth grade. Her persistence and tenacity pulled me through school despite a severe learning disability that no one recognized or understood at that time. It was her determination and perseverance that inspired me as an adult to never ever give up.

And now, I was struggling to understand God's words in the Bible. I loved the Psalms which had some of the easier verses for me to read and understand. There was one in particular that I read over and over for the comfort it gave me.

The Lord says,
"I will rescue those who love me.
I will protect those who trust in my name.
When they call on me, I will answer;
I will be with them in trouble.
I will rescue and honor them.
I will reward them with long life
and give them salvation."

(Psalm 91: 14-16)

That verse was singed into my brain. I could not know then that, one day, I would display this Psalm in plain view for all to see God's promise in His Word.

CHAPTER 6

The Vigil Continues.

P atsy's outlook was bleak according to every doctor who visited, and there were many. The procession of doctors going in and out seemed endless. They all repeated the same negative prognosis for Patsy's recovery. I, in turn, repeated the same positive antidote for her illness... Jesus.

I can only speculate, but I believe that these were not just routine visits. Because Patsy's illness was so rare and so severe, doctors were drawn to the scene both by curiosity and by the hope of learning something new about this mysterious disease.

I remember one female doctor from India whom I had never seen before. After viewing Patsy and her medical charts, she turned and spoke to me. After explaining how rare this illness was, she spoke about the severity of Patsy's case. In her opinion, it was almost certain that if Patsy lived, she would need constant care and be permanently bedridden.

I suspect she knew that I had been telling everyone how Patsy would be healed and was trying to prepare me for the worst. She probably also thought I was a nut case. Her statement did not even faze me. Still fresh in my mind were the words God had spoken to me.

"Doctor," I said, "there are some things that can only be explained by God's healing power, and this is going to be one of them. Jesus is going to heal my wife, completely."

"It's good that you have faith," she replied, "but I'm afraid it won't help with this illness."

"God and faith are beyond our understanding," I answered. "What we can see with our own eyes may be far different from what God has hidden from our view. I can see how Patsy looks, but I also know what God can do, and he will heal her... because He said so." This became one of my constant prayers: "Lord, don't let me judge by my eyes, but by your Living Word."

Many of our friends and members of our church came to visit during that time. I continued to proclaim God's message — that Patsy would be healed. I was told later by a good friend from my church that there was a lot of doubt about Patsy being healed and also about my sanity. I am glad I didn't know it at the time. Although my faith in God's words never wavered, I still needed the emotional support of friends and family. God brings His people together, doubting or not, to give comfort. He can use anyone or anything to deliver his message or to further his purpose.

I was sitting in the ICU visitor's area so family and friends could visit Patsy in her coma state. While I was sitting there, I received a call from David, a man who worked for the dealership where I bought most of my cars. I answered the phone, knowing who it was.

"David, how are you?" I thought he might have heard about Patsy, but he hadn't.

"Ron, I just found out that the new model change is coming up for 2007, and I was wondering if you wanted to purchase one for your wife."

He knew I usually bought a new car every year or two. I didn't say anything about Patsy, but I thought for a minute. *"Expect the miracle! You already have confirmation from God."*

Then I said, "David, go ahead and order it."

"Ron," he said, "I know you're a great customer, but company policy says I have to collect a five-hundred-dollar deposit."

"Sure," I said. I pulled out my wallet and gave him my credit card number. "When do the new models arrive?"

"They'll be here in mid-November."

"Make it the midnight blue with the tan interior, Patsy's favorite color combination."

I can say now, without any doubt, that I believed Patsy was going to drive that car home. But it was only by the grace God had given me to trust in His almighty power. So I finally knew what grace is. Grace is something that only God can give you. He chose to give me grace through His words, "Ron, this is not about you. This is about Me." With grace comes faith. He said, "Your wife will be healed." And I finally believed Him.

Now, I needed to go back to Atlanta. Some business matters had come up which only I could handle. So I flew home and went to the office. I walked into the offices of each of my key people, asking them to join me in the conference room. I knew I needed to give them assurances that everything was going to be okay. Patsy had been a key player in the company, and she left a big void.

I know that uncertainty can be very destructive to the morale of a company. I could feel the anxiety in the room and could almost hear their thoughts and worries: *"How will this impact the company? What will happen to me... to my job... to my family?"*

Fear can be deadly. I was filled with emotion as I gathered my thoughts. *"How can I explain this without sounding nuts? After all, how many people have actually heard God speak directly to them?"* Yet I knew it was essential to restore their confidence.

I spoke to the group saying, "I know you must all be very concerned for Patsy. You've heard about the severity of her illness. You've probably heard how she looks from some of the people who have gone to see her. But people can be too quick to judge by what they see with their eyes, instead of listening to the Living Word of God. And I can tell you that God spoke directly to me, and He said that He would heal her." (2 Corinthians 5:7) *"For we live by believing and not by seeing."*

I could feel the sudden tension in the room, and I imagined my employees thinking, "We'd better get a doctor for Ron, or we'll lose him too."

"I know how that sounds," I continued. "I realize that you could think I imagined it, but I didn't." I went on to tell the story about how God spoke to me, what He said, and how He timed it to make sure I knew it was Him and no one else. As I looked into their eyes, I could see the empathy for me along with their worry for my mental state.

I have no doubt that everyone in the room wanted to believe what I said, but I could see there was a lot of skepticism. We all have a hard time believing something out of the ordinary unless we see or hear it for ourselves. That's when our faith is really tested. But even seeing or hearing does not bring you the faith you need to endure and believe. Only God's grace can do that.

It reminded me of how Peter's faith was tested. Peter had seen Jesus perform all kinds of miracles, and Peter thought his own faith was unbreakable. But Jesus had warned Peter that he would deny Him three times that night... and Peter did. The story tells us that seeing is not always believing. It was only later, through God's grace, that Peter had the faith and courage to be crucified upside down because he felt he was unworthy to be crucified like Christ. It is God's grace that gives us faith, courage, and the strength to resist temptation.

After the meeting, they all came up and hugged me. I advised them to trust, not me, but God.

Later, I left the office to run some personal errands and get a bite to eat. It was lunchtime, and I stopped at a restaurant close to my office. As I was walking in, I recognized someone I didn't expect to see in this neck of the woods as she was a long way from home. She was not someone I had known well, but, as soon as she saw me, she ran up to me and hugged me very affectionately. She said that she had heard about Patsy and was so sorry.

"Thank you, Jolene (as I will call her). It's going to be all right. Jesus is going to heal Patsy."

She smiled, "Are you by yourself?"

"Yes, I am."

"Are you having lunch here?" she asked. "I was going to try it out. Let's have lunch together."

After we went in and sat down, she started to tell me how good I looked, noticing that I had lost some weight. I thanked her for the compliment and assumed she was just being nice. Over lunch, she began to tell me about her love life — how empty it was and how she wished she could find someone like me. I told her that there are plenty of good guys out there and that I have my own issues as everybody else does. I was starting to get a little uneasy at this point. But I still didn't think too much about it.

As the conversation continued, she said she would like to help me. She offered to come over and cook for me and give me comfort during this tough time. Now, I must tell you, Jolene was one beautiful woman — and she knew I was wealthy and, just maybe, about to be single. By this point, it was becoming obvious that she was not just expressing friendly concern, and I was pretty sure of her intentions. Unfortunately, my biggest weakness has always been beautiful women, and, like most guys would be, I was sorely tempted.

I knew I needed to get out of there pretty quickly, or I might find myself in big trouble. I thanked her and told her it was not necessary for her to come over as my neighbors and friends were bringing me food. Still, she insisted that she wanted to come over and help me. It hit me then how lonely I had been, and how much I craved the comfort that intimacy brings.

With all the moral courage I had at that time, I said..."Well, let me see how things are tonight, and I will let you know."

In the Bible, Paul talks about the things he wants to do that he doesn't, and the things he doesn't want to do that he does (see Romans 7:15-20). I was in one of those dilemmas. I fought the lust of my body and the aching loneliness of my heart. The temptation was so great that it was beginning to overwhelm my judgment. I needed to leave... immediately!

I jumped into my car and started praying for God's help. If I did what I wanted to do at that moment, my whole testimony would be a complete sham... saying how much I loved my wife... saying that God had spoken to me and was going to heal her. I could not have lived with myself.

I went straight to my church. I was hoping my pastor Thomas would be there so I could pray with him. As always, God's timing was perfect. He was there, and I was relieved. My spirit had been weakening as I was driving to the church. I went to Thomas 'office, closed the door, and told him what had just happened, and he counseled with me. My pastor at that time was a fairly young man, but he was very wise and had excellent biblical knowledge. Before I left we prayed for God's protection.

As I was driving home, I realized I should not be alone. I went to my neighbor's house and stayed late into the night, not saying a word about what had transpired. I think I didn't say anything because I was afraid of the repercussions if my resolve failed. I finally went home and took some sleeping pills so I could sleep and keep Jolene and the lunch conversation out of my head.

I didn't feel the hand of Satan that time. I truly believe God was protecting me. It was the greatest temptation I could ever recall. Right then, I was so vulnerable that Satan could have had a field day with me, but for the Hand of God protecting me.

The next morning, I decided to go back to Raleigh early. I needed to get away from here as I feared I would succumb to temptation. I changed my flight and went back early. I thanked God for his grace. I would not have had the strength to resist that temptation without Him.

It was January 30, and Patsy had been on the Star Wars machine for almost nine days. There is a limit to how long anyone can stay on that machine. Necessary as it may be, it is very hard on your body which will eventually be weakened beyond repair. They told me that Patsy would be coming off the machine tomorrow.

They had done all they could for her. Now we would just have to wait and see if Patsy was capable of sustaining life without life support, and how much damage the virus had done to Patsy's brain. Again, they told me her outlook was very bleak.

"You don't need to worry," I told the doctors. "Jesus is going to heal her, and I mean fully heal her!"

I could see they really hoped I was right. One of the doctors commented that he had seen God's work before and had seen a few miracles.

"Doc," I said, "this is going to be another one you can add to your list."

Patsy was going to be admitted to step-down ICU. She would no longer have someone constantly by her side. I could not leave her alone in her helpless state, but neither could I stay with her all the time. I needed to find someone with the temperament of an angel — to love her and care for her, and the instincts of a momma grizzly — to protect her and fight for her to the last drop of blood. I knew the person. The question was, would she come?

Patsy and I were very close to Patsy's former husband, Jerry, and his second wife, Linda. Linda was one of the sweetest, most caring, most selfless women I have ever known. Patsy and I both felt that it was important to have a good relationship with our extended families for the sake of our children. With Linda and Jerry, it was easy. They were both great people.

I used to kid with him, "Jerry, you need to start a business picking wives for future husbands. You pick the sweetest women."

Linda was an angel. Several years back, Linda had taken care of Jerry, who nearly died as a result of pneumonia. Her dedication and support were unwavering as she nursed her husband back to health. Later, after our daughter Erica had flipped her SUV and broken both of her feet, Linda came all the way from Houston, Texas, to our home to take care of Erica and her two children.

A year later, Linda was called upon again to take care of her sister who had lupus. Linda had already given her sister a great gift of love — her kidney. But, after all the years of battling cancer, her sister had succumbed to the illness. Linda cared for her sister full-time in her final days. I knew that Linda was the one.

So I called her and said, "Linda, I'm going to ask something of you that I know is a lot to ask. Patsy is moving to the Step-Down ICU unit at Duke Hospital tomorrow, but she is still terribly fragile. I just can't leave her alone, but I also have a company to run. Would you be willing to come and be her daytime helper and companion? I've hired a nursing team to be with her at night, but I need someone I totally trust to be with her during the day."

I could feel the hesitation before she even spoke. Linda replied very solemnly, "Ron, I don't think I have what it takes to help Patsy."

"Linda, you do have what it takes. It's your great love for people." I asked her to pray about it, and she said she would.

I was hoping and praying that she would come. It would take a great sacrifice for both Linda and Jerry. Linda would have to quit her job and be away from her two grandchildren who were both in their formative years. They lived on a large property with farm animals — goats, a horse, and other animals that required daily care. If she were to come, all the work would land squarely on Jerry's shoulders. Was I asking too much? I waited anxiously for her call, but she did not call back... not that day or the next.

The next day was January 31, and Patsy was going to be disconnected from the Star Wars machine and moved to the ICU Step-Down Unit. There, the staff was hoping she would begin to wake up, providing that she could sustain life on her own. They needed to get her set up in the new room before I could see her again.

I took my last look at Patsy before I left the room. She had been through a lot. This machine, as good as it was, had taken a toll on her body. She had no muscle tone. Her body was swollen from all the fluids, and her complexion was like a white sheet with absolutely no color to her skin.

Seeing how she looked, her body lying there so lifeless, I would have said, "There is no way,"... except for God's gift of faith. I had to keep reminding myself of God's words, *"It's not about you, Ron. It's about Me. And your wife will be healed.*" Those are the words I clung to. Through it all, they were my lifeline.

Finally, it was time. It was a solemn walk down the long hallway to Patsy's room. I was thinking about her and hoping she would look a little better. I walked slowly into her room, hoping and praying again that she would be awake. As I walked to the foot of her bed, I could see the stillness of her feet under the hospital sheet. My hope that she would be awake had just been wishful thinking.

As I raised my eyes toward her head, I could see the marks that the IV's had left behind. Her arms and parts of her lower neck were all black and blue. Then I noticed all the wires hooked up to her head. They were monitoring not just her heart and vital signs; they were also monitoring her brain waves. And she was still in a coma.

There is something about the number three. When God sends a message or expresses his will through people, he seems to use them in threes. I had been told on three different occasions by three different people to take pictures of Patsy in her coma state. I had mentioned it to someone who said they thought it was a sign from God. But I just brushed it aside for a time while she was hooked to the Star Wars machine. Eventually, I began to think that what they said might be true.

A few days after she went to Step-Down, I finally took my first picture of Patsy, never knowing that I would write this book, and the picture would become a part of it. In the picture, Patsy is still in a coma with all those wires pasted to her head, monitoring her brain waves.

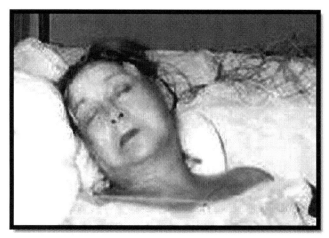

Patsy, Wired to Monitors

I spent several anxious days, waiting and hoping that Linda would call and say, "Yes!" By that time, my ADHD was kicking in at full throttle, triggering deep anxiety. When the call finally came, Linda said, "I will come and do my best. That's all I can promise, and I'm also not sure how long I can stay." Her answer was like hearing angels singing.

"Linda, I don't care how long you come for. Every day that you are here will be one day that I know Patsy will be loved and cared for. It will put me at ease when I have to be in Atlanta." It would be two long weeks before Linda could get all her affairs in order and come.

Once again it was time to wait — one of the hardest things for those with ADHD. My daughter Julie came to be with me during this time. She was in the medical field and took a leave of absence to help monitor Patsy's care until Linda arrived. Julie is also a persistent individual. I guess it runs in the family. We would man the day shift together — 8 a.m. to 8 p.m.

I hired a nursing staff company to have a nurse at Patsy's bedside, monitoring her care, from 8 p.m. to 8 a.m. the next morning. The nurses who came to be with Patsy were God sent. They were angels sent from heaven — all wonderful Christian women. One of them, named Harriet, keeps in contact with us to this day. They played Christian music for her, they read the Bible to her every night, and they constantly prayed at her bedside. I felt the comforting peace of God's presence in that room.

But peace was not what I was to have. The staff was struggling to manage Patsy's constantly spiking body temperature. There was still some infection left, which they were battling with more anti-viral drugs along with heavy doses of Tylenol to keep the high temperature at bay. And she was still in a coma.

It was a very tense time. Even though I knew that God was going to heal her, my emotions were in chaos. I kept going back and forth in my head between the reality I had seen with my eyes and the reality I had heard in God's words to me. It was a battle that could only be won by God's grace.

The heat of the battle turned up as they found a blood clot in Patsy's stomach, and she also began to contract pneumonia, caused by aspirating substances from her feeding tube. The battle grew even more heated as she came down with another illness called C.-diff (short for Clostridium difficile). C.-diff is an infection caused by too many antibiotics given to someone in too short a time. This alone can be enough to kill someone.

The doctors seemed to look grimmer each day. With all the complications that were arising, they did not encourage me to hope for Patsy's survival. I thank God that Julie was there, keeping the staff aware of all Patsy's complications and making sure she received prompt attention.

One day, while I was back in Atlanta, I got a call from Julie. She told me that Patsy was battling to keep her blood-oxygen level up. It had dropped below the normal level as a result of the pneumonia. If it continued to fall, it could cause organ failure as well as brain damage.

Then she said, "Dad, I have to ask you something that the hospital wants to know."

Julie paused and started to cry. "They wanted to know if you would want to allow DNR."

I asked Julie what DNR was. She paused again and burst into tears, blurting out, "Do not resuscitate."

Those words were an assault on the center of my core. I was silenced for a moment. I thought about Gods words. (Isaiah 40:31) *But those who trust in the Lord will find new strength. They will soar high on wings like eagles. They will run and not grow weary. They will walk and not faint.* It took all I had to control my emotions while waiting for Julie to gain control of hers. Julie already knew my answer, but needed to verify it. I confirmed it for her.

"Julie, you tell the hospital not just NO! You tell them, ABSOLUTELY, UNEQUIVOCALLY, NO!"

I was completely overcome by that news. My body wanted to explode. I flopped down on the bed, wanting the pain to go away and praying that prayer over and over. "Lord, don't let me judge by my eyes, but by your living word." I had to stay focused on the promise God made when he spoke to me.

Trust in the Lord with all your heart;
Do not depend on your own understanding.

(Proverbs 3:5)

After a long while, the prayers began to bring me a measure of relief. (James 5:15) *"Such a prayer offered in faith will heal the sick, and the Lord will make you well."* I lay there, exhausted, watching the sun dip toward the horizon, my mind drifting to thoughts of Patsy... of the way we met, the way we lived, and the way our love bound us together.

CHAPTER 7

Patsy and Me – We Were
Meant to Be

I met Patsy in March of 1985. I was at a nightclub with a couple of friends from work, and Patsy and a girlfriend were at another table close by. It was apparent from the way they were watching the people on the dance floor that they were anxious to dance, and so was I.

Now I must tell you, I am no Fred Astaire... more like twinkle toes Fred Flintstone. I had two left feet that always wanted to go right. But I also knew that dancing was a prerequisite to mingling and having fun. So I finally worked up the nerve to get up and walk over to their table, hoping I would not get a brush-off.

They were both attractive women, but Patsy had really caught my eye. With my heart in my throat, I looked at her and said, "Would you like to dance?"

She looked up at me with a smile that lit up the room and said, "Yes, I WOULD!!!"

Patsy's smile just threw me back for a second. I had never before seen anyone smile so exuberantly at just being asked to dance. She radiated glowing warmth like nothing I had ever experienced. Her smile seemed to say, "I am already in love with you." And she didn't even know my name. Patsy would later say that she fell in love with me, at first sight, that night.

We headed for the dance floor and started rock 'n' rolling to the fast beat. Luckily, that was something I could do because there are no set moves and pretty much anything goes. So my two left feet went right or left, or in any sequence they desired. That's the beauty of rock 'n' roll. We had been dancing for less than a minute when Patsy went into her "ask-question" mode.

"So what's your sign?" she asked.

"Virgo," I answered.

"I'm a Virgo too!" Patsy replied with her dazzling smile. "Are you married?"

"NO!" I answered. "I've been there and done that. I'm divorced."

"Me too," she said. "Do you have kids?"

"Yes, I have three daughters."

"I have a daughter, too!" she exclaimed. "How old are your kids?"

"The oldest is eleven," I answered. "My middle girl is eight, and the little one is six."

"My daughter is eleven," she added with a big smile. "Just like your oldest!"

Then she asked me, "How long have you been divorced?"

Now, this was beginning to get a little too personal for my own comfort. I had just been through a very difficult and complex divorce. My emotions had gone through the wringer along with my pocketbook, and I needed time for my wounds to heal and my wallet to re-inflate. Divorce was the last thing I wanted to think or talk about. I just wanted to get out, have some fun, and meet some new people.

I thought for a minute and then asked myself, "*Is she going to write a book about me?*" Who knew that one day I would be writing a book about HER? God knew!

I smiled and said, "You ask too many questions for a first dance." Patsy just smiled back, and we kept on dancing.

Now, I have always been a very sociable person, and I like to be out and about. However, at this juncture of my life, I did not want any part of a serious relationship. Patsy seemed to me to be lining up our relationship with the stars.

But, she was as radiant as the evening stars, drop-dead gorgeous, and unbelievably sweet. She reminded me of an M&M with its smooth, flawless candy shell that wraps around the sweet chocolate beneath. I was enchanted. So, for the rest of the night, Patsy and I danced and chatted... but with no more questions.

We were sitting and talking when the slow dance was announced. I was debating whether to ask her to dance. I was starting to like Patsy, and I was afraid the slow dance would make me want to like her even more. Although I did want to fall in love again someday, now was not the time. I needed to heal my wounds first so I wouldn't carry them into the next relationship. Patsy was the type one could easily get serious with.

Also, I was very self-conscious about my two left feet. I hadn't danced with someone I didn't know in a long time, so I was feeling a little nervous. I was wondering, *"Can I get one foot to go right? Do I hold her hands out in front of us or to the side? Do I hold her shoulder and one of her hands? Do I wrap my arms around her back or her waist?"*

Yet, I was having a great time, and Patsy's glow and sweetness just drew me in. So I turned to her nervously and asked, "Would you like to dance?"

You would have thought I was asking her if she would like a ten thousand dollar check. Without the slightest hesitation, she was on her feet, holding out her hands, giving me that vivacious smile, and answering, "ABSOLUTELY!"

You don't get more direct than that. What I learned to love about Patsy was her honesty, her directness, and her innocence. I once called Patsy on the phone and said, "Patsy, get ready. We are going to your favorite restaurant."

"Hot diggity dog!" she blurted out with delight. Those were the cutest, most innocent, three words I had ever heard… three words that I will never forget.

So Patsy and I walked onto the dance floor and proceeded to slow dance. When she looked at me with those mesmerizing blue eyes, one of my left feet instantly became a right foot, and my arms just naturally went where they were supposed to. Her eyes told me what to do.

Later, I would coin that indescribable look as "goo-goo eyes." When I looked into her eyes, I saw all the warmth and love of people that she projected. At that moment, it was all aimed right at me. I had never had anyone look at me like that before. It made for a completely magical dance.

With Patsy, my feet were moving like I'd had a leg transplant, and John Travolta was the donor. She made me feel completely at ease and no longer awkward… like a real man. It was wonderful, and my intuition had been right on. I liked her even more after the dance.

It was time to leave, and so we exchanged business cards. I took Patsy's card and placed it deep within my wallet. Guys, you know all about the business cards you have in your wallet that you never look at until it's time for a new wallet. I went home that night, thinking about Patsy, but convincing myself, "*I don't want to get into a relationship right now.*" So that's the reason why I buried the card in my wallet.

Days and weeks had gone by. I would think about Patsy from time to time, but I was determined not to get too involved. Patsy was the type of girl you would want to marry, but I was not going to allow my thoughts to drive that train. And, gradually, I did stop thinking about her.

About a month had gone by. My sister Vickie was living with me to share the rent and utility costs. Divorces are very expensive both emotionally and financially.

One night, when I came home from work, my sister said, "Ronnie, some girl named Pat Jackson called for you. She said she was a real estate agent, and she had some property she wanted to show you."

I was puzzled. "Real estate? Pat Jackson?"

"Ronnie," my sister said. "You have to be kidding! You don't have two nickels to rub together. How can you even think about buying property?"

"Don't worry, Vickie. I'm not buying anything," I said as I drifted off, loosening my tie and heading for my room. I was racking my brain trying to think, "Pat Jackson—who is she?"

Then it dawned on me. It must be Patsy. I dug down into my wallet to check the name and found her card. Sure enough, it said Pat Jackson.

"Now why would she call me and say that?" I was too curious to let it go, so I called her. Patsy answered the phone. Just hearing her voice gave me a butterfly tingle... the kind you get only when you really like someone.

"Hey, this is Ron Tripodo," I said. "My sister told me you called."

"OH!!! THAT'S YOUR SISTER!!!" Patsy responded. "I wasn't sure if it was your girlfriend, or maybe your former wife." I had to really laugh when she said that.

Still laughing, I said, "Is that why you said you wanted to show me some property?"

Patsy laughed. "Yes!" she said.

She went on to tell me that she'd had such a great time the night we met, and she wanted to talk to me again. I told her I'd had a great time as well, and I had thought about her too.

Now at the time, I didn't have much money. And that's an understatement. I wanted to ask her out, but I had "elephant ears." That's when you reach into your pockets to check for money, and both pockets are empty. So then you pull your pockets out, and they are hanging outside your pants like elephant ears. I could only afford to visit her or maybe drive around in the car, but there was no money to take her to dinner or a movie. I didn't want her to think I was a bum. So I didn't ask her.

We talked for a while, and I said I hoped that I would see her again. When I hung up the phone, I had mixed feelings. I really wanted to ask her out, but the embarrassment of elephant-ear syndrome convinced me otherwise.

Several weeks went by, and my thoughts of Patsy were diminishing. I was making dinner for a girl that I worked with, whom I kind of liked, although there were no fireworks blazing. As we were eating, I heard a knock on the door. I wondered who it could be. I got up, went to the door, and opened it. There was Patsy looking hotter than a steel-melting furnace.

My first reaction was, "Wow, come on in!"

But then I realized that I had another girl in my apartment. You want to talk about one of those awkward moments? Well, I was having one.

I said to Patsy, "I would like to invite you in, but I have someone here right now. How did you find my address anyhow?"

"Being a real estate agent has its advantages. I just cross-referenced your phone number to get your address,"

"You can do that?" I asked, surprised.

"I do it all the time to get listings," she answered. "You can also do it in reverse. You can use an address to get a phone number." You have to remember... this was back in the days before cell phones when everyone had a landline, and your contact list was the phone book.

"I'll give you a call," I said, "and maybe you can tell me more about the real estate business... and maybe show me some property." We both laughed.

Several weeks passed, and, instead of Patsy receding from my thoughts, she was monopolizing them. I couldn't get her out of my head. I had never had anyone chase me before, and it felt good. In the past, I was always the one doing the chasing. I knew I didn't have much money to take her out, so I racked my brains to find something we could do that wouldn't cost much, but wouldn't make me appear cheap. It occurred to me that I could tell her about my work in the construction business and offer to show her around my world. It would be a great way to break the ice.

You talk about a fish story. This is more like a whale story! I had no authority at all in the site selection process. I was just a project manager over a few apartment complexes that were being built. But it would cost nothing to give her a grand tour. It was the perfect idea. I could go out with Patsy and stay within my budget... or so I thought.

So I called Patsy. She answered the phone, and I said, "This is Ron."

In her bubbly, jubilant voice she exclaimed, "HOW ARE YOU? I am SO glad you called me!"

I was thinking to myself, "Wow! Is it me, or is she like this with everybody?" Later, after I took Patsy to Cleveland to meet my parents, my mom told my sister, "That Patsy is just TOO sweet! There has to be something wrong with her."

But Patsy was and is that sweet. She made me feel so wanted, so accepted, and she really didn't even know me yet. Talking with Patsy was like sinking down into a soft cushiony favorite armchair. I was totally at ease. So I told her my idea.

"Absolutely!" she said enthusiastically. I could feel the warm smile all the way through the telephone line. "That's a great idea. Let's do it!"

Later, I found that she too was giving me a whale of a fish story. Back then she'd had no experience in commercial property listings or sales. Besides that, she'd only had her license for a few months. We were both fishing for a way to get together.

On our first date, I was going to take Patsy out and show her some of the building sites that I was working on. I had picked her up on a Saturday afternoon, and we had a great time traveling to the different construction sites. The afternoon had flown by, and it was turning into early evening. I was almost sure Patsy was getting hungry because I sure was.

There wasn't much left from my last paycheck, and I had to get through the next week before I would get paid again. I really wanted to take her to dinner and NOT to a hamburger joint. But, at that time, it would have cost twenty-five to thirty dollars for a good dinner at a fairly nice place. That would take most of my gas and food money for the week ahead. I didn't want to look cheap. I was beginning to really like Patsy, and I wanted to make a good impression. So I blocked out the thought of having to push my car and eat ramen noodles for the week.

"Would you like to go to dinner?" I asked.

Patsy looked at me, and her eyes lit up. But, being her sweet, considerate self, Pasty said, "Oh, you don't have to take me to dinner."

With a very confident voice, I said, "I know I don't have to. I want to."

That said, with her bubbly, charming voice, Patsy answered, "I would LOVE to!"

When I heard the word "love" come out of her mouth, it made my heart skip a beat. I felt as though I had never heard that word before. And I wanted to hear it again.

So we went to dinner, we shared stories that made us laugh, and we realized how much we had in common. By the time we left, most of the other customers were long gone.

As I drove Patsy back to her house, I was thinking that I would really like to kiss her. Guys and gals all know the usual ritual on the first date when you like someone. Although I longed for that kiss, I also wanted to be a gentleman and not look too pushy. So, in that awkward moment, I told her that I would call her and that she could let me know if she finds any property.

As I said good night to Patsy, she looked right at me with her goo-goo eyes that seemed to say, "I love you Ron Tripodo." I was mesmerized. For a moment I was paralyzed as I felt all my senses exploding in a cascade of bells and stars. I was trying so hard not to show it. It was taking every ounce of my power to refrain. But, I just couldn't resist. I had to kiss her, and I did. That's when the overheat alarm system went off in my head… the kiss was that unforgettable!!

And at that, Patsy said, "Good night Ron. I had a wonderful time. It was so much fun. I hope I will see you again."

Later, Patsy told me that was the best kiss she ever had in her life. No one had ever told me before that I was their best kiss. Patsy was the best kiss I'd ever had as well. Patsy still talks about that kiss to me even to this day. When she does, I always ask her, "Can I get that best kiss again?" My wonderful Patsy!

But the next day and the next, I couldn't get her goo-goo eyes out of my head. I wanted to call her, but I didn't want to look too anxious. I knew it was not a good idea to start up a relationship that would very likely become more than "just good friends." Still, I desperately wanted to see her again. What a dilemma!

I debated back and forth in my mind. Patsy was incredible. She was a completely different type of girl from any that I had dated before. Could she be the one? Was Patsy my destiny?

I had to risk it. So I called her, and Patsy and I started seeing each other. I didn't know then, but I do know now that Patsy and I WERE meant for each other... like the card from our nineteenth anniversary: "You and me... were meant to be."

As anyone knows who has been in love, it's euphoric. For the first time in my life, I truly felt it with my whole being. It wasn't just physical. It was much, much more. It was the whole enchilada. I was finally learning what love really is. Love is the greatest gift God has bestowed on His children... His love for us, our love for Him, and the love we have for each other.

Love is something that is beyond my ability to fully explain. Love is about the other person, and that other person's love is about you. True love is total unselfishness towards each other. Love is devotion to the other person's well-being without even needing to think about it, measure it, or keep score. Love has no conditions set upon it. Love pervades every aspect of your life—like a habit you form that continues to run on automatic pilot. Love is total commitment followed by action and patience.

When two people are in sync with love, it is the strongest bond in the world. Love is the glue needed for any marriage, blended family, or relationship to endure. No matter how old you are, the spark that lit the flame of love between the two of you will never die... as long as you remember why you fell in love with the person who lit that flame.

As my thoughts returned to the present, I was hoping that God would grant His promise soon. The waiting was hard, but reliving the memories of a happier time gave me relief during this dark time.

CHAPTER 8

God's Angel Arrives

T hose first two weeks in Step-Down, I had been riding a roller coaster, not knowing what to expect at the next turn. Patsy's temperature was still not stable, and some of her complications were lingering. But the worst had not happened, and Patsy was beginning to show some hopeful signs.

I was concerned by Patsy's appearance. They had removed all the wires on her head. This created what could be called in the women's world a bad hair day. I wanted her first glimpse of herself in the mirror to make her smile, not cringe.

Now, Patsy has always been very selective about who worked on her hair. There was a man named Jacques, a private vendor working in the hospital to perform at-bedside washing and blow-drying of patients' hair. I figured a hairdresser named Jacques just had to be good. And he was. Patsy slept through the whole salon treatment.

Patsy was also big on keeping her skin moisturized, and I was determined to continue her tradition. I started moisturizing her face, and I mean moisturizing. I slathered on globs of it, figuring the more I used, the better the results — typical male thought, right?

The nurses complained to my daughter Julie that I was putting on way too much, and it was getting all over the nurses and all over the sheets. Guys, we have no idea about moisture creams and, for that matter, no idea about makeup. But, even with a feeding tube up her nose, to me, Patsy looked beautiful.

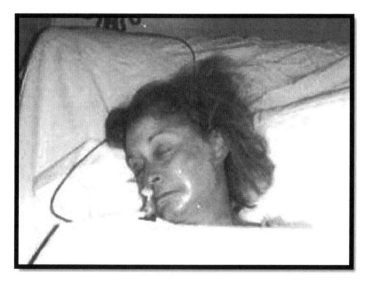

Patsy with Hairdo and Moisturizer

8 – God's Angel Arrives.

It was Sunday, February 12, 2006, and Linda was arriving at the Raleigh airport. I had a lot on my mind that day as I drove to the airport. I didn't want to overwhelm Linda with all of Patsy's complications, but I also wanted to brief her on what was going on so that she would be somewhat equipped to monitor Patsy's care.

On our way to the hospital, I described Patsy's condition and how she had begun to wake up for a few minutes at a time. I also told her how God had spoken to me, saying that Patsy would be healed. I assured her that, no matter what she needed, she would have my full support, and, most of all, God's help as He had promised.

Linda said, "I promise you, Ron, I will do everything I can to help Patsy return to her lovely, vibrant self."

We arrived at the hospital and walked into Patsy's room. Rather than a look of shock or dismay, Linda's face showed only loving concern and determination. She was clearly no stranger here. Linda went straight to Patsy's bed and began to rub her forehead.

Linda looked up. "Ron, she has a slight temperature."

Julie, who had been sitting with Patsy, said, "It's starting to stabilize. It's better than it has been. It's averaging a little below a hundred degrees. Before, it was a couple of degrees higher."

Linda was already digging in for the fight. Her momma grizzly instincts were kicking in. She had some remedies for Patsy's temperature and took over from Julie with cold, wet compresses for Patsy's forehead. She ordered a fan for the room and asked the nurse for a special type of sheet that would keep Patsy cool.

Right then I could see that Linda was "the one." Linda was a fighter, and that's what Patsy would need. My heart was suddenly lighter, and I was filled with gratitude.

Linda settled in and, along with the night nurses, gave Patsy the best care imaginable. Patsy would now wake up for five minutes at a time, several times a day. When she woke up, she would sometimes look at Linda or me and just stare. She had no idea who we were, or where she was, or what was happening to her.

It was a hard time for me, especially now, since it was February 14, Valentine's Day. My heart yearned for a romantic dinner with the love of my life in some dimly lit restaurant where the waiter's name is unpronounceable and the check is astronomical.

Of course, it would not be possible this year. Patsy would be eating through a tube, and I would be grabbing whatever from the hospital cafeteria. But I also knew for certain that we would have that dinner someday.

I remembered in times past how Patsy always loved it when I would bring her a stuffed animal. Her eyes would shine with delight as she hugged it close. It brought out the innocent little girl in Patsy. I cherished that part of her.

So I went downstairs and found a pink-and-red teddy bear holding a heart with the word "LOVE" embroidered on it. I knew Patsy would love it, and I bought it.

When I came back to the room, Patsy was lying there so peacefully, like an angel sleeping on a cloud. I wanted to crawl in next to her and just hold her. Of course, I couldn't. So the next best thing was to lay the bear down beside her, pretending that it was me.

The Bear I Wished Was Me

After Linda had been there for a week, Patsy would sometimes stay awake for as long as an hour or two at a time. But there was something wrong. Now that she was awake longer, we could clearly tell that she was not moving her right arm or leg, and the right side of her face was drooping. We found out that she was completely paralyzed on the right side, much like a stroke victim.

It was a disheartening setback. My resolve to stay on the faith track was being tested, and I knew that prayer would be the only thing to prevent a wipe-out on that track. Once again, I reached out to my family, my friends, and my church to ask for their prayers. I let them know what was happening so they would know what to pray for.

Now, you might wonder — if I was so sure that God would heal Patsy, then why was I asking for prayers? Why didn't I just sit around and wait? Had I perhaps lost faith?

The answer to that is an emphatic *NO*. My faith never wavered, but it was sorely tested. I was tortured by each setback, not because of doubt, but because of the anxiety of not knowing: not knowing how or when God would act; not knowing what God wanted me to do; but, most of all, not being able to handle my own impatience. I had to trust Him no matter what I saw or what I felt.

I believe very strongly in the power of prayer. When we pray to God, we also honor Him with our trust, and we acknowledge that He is real and all-powerful. This gives us the strength to endure adversity. With prayer comes praise and gratitude; they go hand and hand. To me, bringing all these other voices to echo my own prayers, was something I could do for God — perhaps the only thing.

One morning, soon after the prayers, Linda was in the room alone with Patsy. I was downstairs talking on the phone. When I came back to the room, Linda was in tears. She said, "Patsy moved her right arm!"

"What?"

"I was sitting next to her," said Linda, "when, all of a sudden, she lifted her right arm and scratched the right side of her face."

I was jubilant. All I could hear were those words: *"Your wife will be healed."* At that moment, I realized what a difference a day or two can make when God is at work. I needed to take one day at a time and trust God. I needed to keep praying for the strength to get me through to the next day.

I ran and told the nurses and doctors who were on staff. They came into the room and wanted to see her do it again. Patsy could not yet understand commands and did not move her arm or her leg.

Later that day while Linda and I were in the room, she moved her right leg. Again, I ran and told the nurses and doctors what had happened. Once again, they came in and tried to get Patsy to move her arm and leg, but she still couldn't understand what they wanted her to do.

I suppose the staff thought we were just imagining it. This went on for several days, but the only time she moved her right side was when Linda and I were alone in the room with her.

Then one day, I was asked to meet with the hospital coordinator who facilitates the future care of patients. Linda and I sat down with her, and she explained that there wasn't much more they could do for Patsy at Duke. I needed to go back to Atlanta and find Patsy a sub-acute care facility.

I don't remember exactly what she said, but it took me by surprise. I had thought they would let Patsy stay longer to recover, so I didn't understand. What I did hear – loud and clear — was the expectation that Patsy wasn't going to get much better and needed a place that deals with the helpless and the hopeless.

I said with all the confidence I could muster that Jesus was going to heal Patsy and that she would not be there long. She wished me well and gave me the names of some of the facilities to check out.

So I flew back to Atlanta. The first facility I visited was horrid. I had never seen conditions like this before. It was cluttered, and the quarters were very tight. It was like storing sick people in a warehouse just waiting for them to die. The next two places weren't much different. I was feeling very discouraged... not knowing what to do because the options I had seen were so bleak. I knew I didn't have the answer, but God did.

CHAPTER 9

Trusting God No Matter What

I was sitting there, wondering what God wanted me to do when the phone rang. The call was from a good friend, Angie, who was also my real estate agent. She wanted to check on Patsy. I said that Patsy had started to move her right side and that all our prayers were being answered.

Then, I mentioned the trouble I was having trying to find a place for Patsy to recover. She told me about a place in Atlanta — Shepherd Center. A friend's son had gone there with a spinal injury, and she was sure they had a brain injury facility, as well.

I immediately looked up Shepherd Center's address and drove there. I was directed to the admissions director's office. She offered to show me around the facility, and I agreed. As I inspected each of the impressive treatment areas, I could see that this was where Patsy needed to be. We went back to her office and sat down.

I started to tell the director about what Patsy had contracted and the care she had received at Duke. I said that Duke had referred me to several sub-acute facilities, but that what Patsy really needed was a rehab center like Shepherd where she could recover completely.

The director began to question me about Patsy's current condition, and I could see the sad look on her face. She said they had seen a few cases of HSE, but nothing even close to Patsy's in severity. She would have to meet certain criteria to be accepted into Shepherd's program. From what I had told her of Patsy's current condition, she didn't think that Patsy could meet the criteria.

I had a hard time hearing those words — those ugly-sounding words. My body was quivering with anxiety. But I knew she was wrong!

I took a deep breath. Then I said, "I understand about the hospital's criteria. But I need to tell you something that will probably sound unbelievable... maybe even insane."

I proceeded to tell her about the incident at the airport. At the end, I said, "God spoke to me out loud and told me with His own voice that He was going to heal her. In fact, His exact words were, 'Your wife will be healed.' He did not say partially healed. He said healed. I believe that He will fully heal her."

The director just stared at me for a moment, saying nothing. Then she said, "We have seen miracles here at Shepherd."

"This will be another one," I said. Then I begged her to reconsider. "I know this is the right place for Patsy. This is the place God has chosen for her. Please accept her."

"It's not that simple," she said. "First, we would have to request Patsy's medical records. Then, we would have to send a nurse up to Duke to evaluate her. Also, we would have to get your insurance company to allow this, or they will not pay for it."

"Ma'am, if the insurance won't cover it, I will. Please send someone up there."

"All right," she finally agreed. "I will see what I can do, but I can make no promises."

As I was leaving, I looked into her eyes. She could see that my heart was hurting. In an emotional voice, I said, "I know that Jesus is going to heal my wife. I know that No One Else Believes me, but God doesn't lie."

I just felt the need to say that. It gave me a sense of security and the assurance of faith that I needed. I thanked her, once again, and told her how much I appreciated her help.

As I drove back to the office, the questions rolled around in my head. *"Will Shepherd take her? Or will God use another way? Or am I just plain nuts? No... definitely not that! I know what I heard."* But I still had to reassure myself over and over, hearing the sound of His words: *"This*

125

is not about you, Ron. It is about Me. And your wife will be healed."

The next day I received a call from Shepherd. They said that they would send a nurse to Duke to evaluate Patsy. Afterwards, they would notify Duke of their decision. I was elated. At the time, I didn't understand why they would call Duke rather than me. Later, I would understand why.

Once more, I had to wait — and the ADHD was kicking in. I had to keep my wits about me, not be overly anxious, be patient, and wait. I was so sure that Shepherd was the perfect place for Patsy. It took two days before I got their answer... two very long days.

It was Friday, February 17. I was sitting in my office finishing up my work for the day when my phone rang. I answered it and was greeted by the coordinator for aftercare from Duke Hospital. She said, "Hello, Mr. Tripodo."

I could sense by the tone of her voice that the news would not be good. "Yes, this is him."

"Mr. Tripodo, I'm afraid the news I have is not very good. Shepherd Center declined to take Patsy."

My heart sank. All the blood in my head rushed to my lower extremities, and I could feel myself starting to lose it. "What did you say?"

Once more, she told me that Shepherd Center had refused to accept Patsy into their care.

"There must be a mistake," I said.

"No, I'm sorry. I confirmed it myself with Shepherd."

I felt as if I had just gotten hit with a baseball bat. The shock! The uncertainty! At that moment, I felt overwhelmed. I just started crying, not understanding what was going on. I knew that God had spoken to me. I knew that He said He was going to heal Patsy. Patsy would have to leave Duke soon, and I was not going to put her in a sub-acute facility. I didn't understand why God wouldn't use Shepherd. Shepherd was perfect. Where else could she go?

Here I was... second guessing God's plan. I needed to have faith, to trust completely. I knew of only one solution to this problem, and that was to pray. God had said He was going to heal Patsy, but He hadn't said how or when. I needed to pray for that.

Jesus said, *"If two of you agree here on earth concerning anything you ask, my Father in heaven will do it for you"* (Matthew 18:19).

I thought to myself, *"If two or more will pray and He will answer, then He would really be honored if we had thousands praying to Him. Is that what He wants me to do?"*

I immediately put together the longest email chain I could assemble. I asked everyone to pray that God would change the minds at Shepherd, or open another door, or just heal Patsy supernaturally. I asked everyone on that chain to contact everyone they knew, and have them, in turn, e-mail everybody they knew to pray for Patsy. (Psalms 6:90) *"The Lord has heard my plea; the Lord will answer my prayer."*

I want to tell you, there were a lot of people praying, all over the country. How could I know that? Well, it happened in a roundabout way. Tom, one of my old friends from the third grade, lived in Cincinnati. His wife Cindy worked for American Airlines in the downtown office. They lived on the east side of the city, and she would commute to work by bus. When you commute, you usually take the same bus at the same time and usually see many of the same people every day.

On the following Monday, February 20, Cindy happened to be sitting next to a woman who was one of the regulars. The woman began to tell her about a lady in Atlanta who was very sick with a brain infection. Her pastor had asked the whole congregation to pray for this lady yesterday in church. Cindy thought for a second and then asked her name. Her answer was, "Patsy Tripodo."

Cindy almost fell off the seat. She couldn't believe how far the prayer chain had reached. She told the woman that she and her husband were very good friends with Patsy and her husband Ron. Right there on the bus, they prayed together for Patsy, praising God for his blessings.

Perhaps that was God's way of saying, "I have heard your prayers, Ron. Trust in Me." I believe that God is always glad to hear from His children and listens to everyone who calls His name.

On the afternoon of that same Monday, I was packing my bags to head back to Duke. A critical business meeting had kept me in Atlanta over the weekend, and I was on edge. I hadn't yet found a facility for Patsy, and I was running out of time. I thought to myself, "What am I going to do?"

When my phone rang, I could see the caller ID. It was Duke. My stomach curled up in a knot. Fearing that something had happened to Patsy, I hurried to answer.

It was the aftercare coordinator, and her voice sounded very upbeat. She said, "I have some great news for you!"

Not knowing what to expect, I froze for a second, gripping the phone with all my might. "What is the good news?"

"You are not going to believe this. All on their own, Shepherd called us back and said they had changed their minds. Shepherd is going to accept Patsy."

I now knew what the trumpets in heaven would sound like. "Please, tell me that one more time," I said.

And she did.

I started hollering, screaming at the top of my lungs, and jumping for joy. I yelled out the words, "Thank You,

Jesus!" Over and over, I just kept yelling, "Thank You, Jesus!"

I was in a state of euphoria. It felt as if the weight of the world had been lifted off my shoulders. The miracle was happening. For Shepherd to call back on their own, with no urging from anyone, and to say they had changed their minds... without any doubt in my mind, that was divine intervention... and the answer to a whole lot of prayers.

Even though I had known that God would heal Patsy in His own way, in His own time, I believed that by asking so many people to lift her up, people who might not have prayed at that moment would do so because of the request. Perhaps they would now honor Him more frequently. People who weren't sure whether God was real might see by His work that He is indeed real. And those who already knew God and believed in Him had one more opportunity to be in His presence.

I believe that God was pleased to hear so many of His people call upon Him, not because they had to, but because they wanted to. Acts like this, done out of love for someone else, bring us closer to God. Through prayers, we can receive His perfect love.

I flew back that afternoon. When I entered Patsy's room, she was alert and smiling as though she knew me. Linda told me that, all day long, Patsy's motor skills had been improving.

There was still a long way to go. She could not talk yet or swallow, and she had to have a feeding tube to eat. She could not understand language to follow commands. But the paralysis on her right side was now completely gone. God had started His work for Patsy's recovery. So that evening we got her up out of bed, and she walked a few steps.

God had answered our prayers. Again, I took comfort from His words in Psalm 91: 14-16.

The Lord says,

> *"I will rescue those who love me;*
> *I will protect those who trust in my name;*
> *When they call on me I will answer;*
> *I will be with them in trouble;*
> *I will rescue and honor them.*
> *I will reward them with long life*
> *and give them salvation."*

Now we had to get Patsy ready for the nearly 400-mile trip from Raleigh to Atlanta. At this point, it was still not safe to move her. But, during the week, the virus finally subsided. The blood clot was gone, along with her pneumonia. They were going to be able to take her IV'S out right before she left for Atlanta.

Because Patsy was unable to swallow food, they needed to perform surgery to permanently attach a feeding tube to her stomach. As they were getting her ready for surgery the nurse explained that the new technology would allow the feeding tube to last for years.

I looked at her and said, "No ma'am, it won't be years. It will be months."

God saw that differently as well.

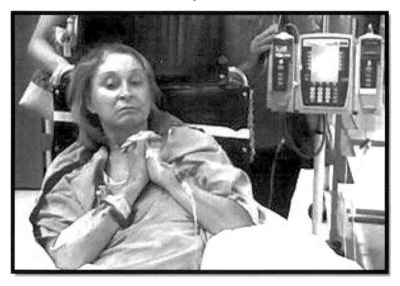

Patsy, Prepared for Surgery to
Insert a Feeding Tube

Finally, the day came when Patsy would start her long trip to Atlanta. With Linda as her protector right by her side, I felt at ease. All the doctors and nurses came to see us off. I could tell by their very warm and gracious goodbyes that they were hoping for a successful ending to this journey home.

Off they went, Patsy and Linda in the ambulance. I watched until they dropped out of view. I was going to catch a plane and be waiting for them when they arrived at Shepherd Center.

Late in the day on February 27, I was eagerly waiting for Patsy and Linda to arrive by ambulance. My anticipation was growing, knowing that Patsy was now home on Georgia soil. They would have been only 20 minutes away if traffic had been light. But rush-hour in Atlanta can be a turkey shoot.

It gave me time to think. I knew that Patsy had a long way to go, and I needed to continue trusting God and keeping the faith. I wondered what would take place next. How would God heal her? What would my role be?

I saw the ambulance pulling into Shepherd's entrance, and I couldn't wait to see Patsy. As they opened the back doors, it was clear that the long trip had drained Patsy both physically and mentally. Linda, too, looked very tired and drained.

They wheeled Patsy inside on a gurney while I went to find a wheelchair with a high back. The paramedics helped me pick Patsy up and place her limp body in the chair. We had to strap her in, so she would not fall forward.

As I was wheeling her to the brain injury unit, a young gentleman asked me, "Is that your mother you're wheeling in?"

"No," I said to him. "It's my wife, and you'd better not let her hear you say that. She will kill you!"

I knew she looked bad, and I was not the only one that could see the wear on her body from that long, exhausting trip. I just wanted to get her checked in as quickly as possible and get her into a room where she could rest.

Patsy still wasn't fully aware of her surroundings and was having a very difficult time staying awake. I kept checking to make sure she was okay. If you had seen her that day, as a few of my friends did, you would have said that there was no way on earth she could kick this. I knew that she couldn't kick it, but I knew that God could and would.

That night I stayed very late, wanting to be with her until the last possible moment. However, Shepherd's policy did not allow visitors to stay the night. In fact, she could have no visitors for the first six days.

Linda and I were both tired. We left, and I finally went home, feeling as though I had left half of myself behind. But, I needed rest as I was to meet with her doctors first thing in the morning. I was on edge, not knowing what they would have to tell me.

CHAPTER 10

The Light at the End
of the Tunnel

I t was February 28. I was on my way to Shepherd, fighting the Atlanta traffic as usual. It gave me time to think of what would come next. How long would it take for Patsy to be healed as God had promised? How long would she be in Shepherd? The nurse at Duke said that the feeding tube was good for years. Would it take years?

I believed in my heart that God was about to speed up the process. Was that just wishful thinking? There were so many questions I could not answer. I knew I couldn't judge by my eyes, I knew I had to judge by His words. I had to trust His words no matter what.

I arrived at Shepherd and walked down the long hallway to Patsy's room. I would meet with the doctors in about 30 minutes, and my daughter Julie was going to join me for the meeting. Her medical background would help me to decipher what they would say. I wanted to make sure that what I heard in this meeting was the same as what she heard. She was already in Patsy's room waiting for me.

The first thing I saw when I walked into the room was Patsy, sleeping like an angel. She looked a little more rested than last night. I kissed her on the forehead, and she woke up. She looked at me, smiled, and said, "Hi."

At Duke, Patsy would try to talk, but it was all gibberish. I couldn't believe it! She spoke to me so clearly. Even though it was only one word, it was a real word, used appropriately. I was so excited. Julie had heard it too, and we both started jumping and shouting for joy. The nurse came in at that moment, alarmed by the shouts until she saw our joyful faces. After we explained what had happened, the nurse smiled and told us that Patsy's night had been restful.

I wanted to stay with Patsy so she would not be afraid of her new surroundings. But Shepherd's policy would not allow that, not for six more days. They wanted her undivided attention, and family could distract her from working on her recovery. I told Patsy I loved her and would be back to see her in a little while. Then Julie and I headed for the conference room.

Before we walked in, I reminded Julie, "No matter what the doctors say, remember that they are just human beings. They don't know what I know. God has promised to heal Patsy."

We walked into the room and sat down. Dr. Kaelin, the head neurologist of the brain injury unit, and a few members of his staff were in the room waiting for us. They asked us to sit down. Dr. Kaelin introduced himself and the staff members.

He then proceeded to tell me that he had examined Patsy and reviewed her medical records. He said, "I must tell you, this girl has been through a lot. The severity of her virus was off the charts. She is lucky to be alive."

"No, Doctor Kaelin," I replied. "Not lucky. She is blessed. God is going to heal her... completely heal her."

"Ron, I hope you're right," he answered. "Because it's going take lots of prayers to get her completely healed. Generally, when the virus is this severe, we don't see a full recovery. Typically, there will be a lifelong disability, and patients usually need to be supervised and require physical help for things like dressing, bathing, and the normal everyday things that we all do."

I listened to what Dr. Kaelin had to say, but it was very hard to hear it all again. I also knew that he was giving me the soft version by using words like "typically" and "generally." It was pretty much the same thing I'd heard before at Duke, and I knew what Patsy was up against — nothing that God couldn't handle.

I said to the doctor, "I want to thank you for accepting Patsy into Shepherd Center. I know she didn't meet the medical criteria to come here. I had been praying along with thousands of people for this to happen, and God answered our prayers."

Then, I told him that God had actually spoken to me and told me He was going to heal Patsy. You never know what kind of reaction you will get when you make a statement like that to someone you don't know. But, in this case, it was received very well. Dr. Kaelin was a godly man, and I was sure he would be praying for Patsy too.

We all went down to Patsy's room. Dr. Kaelin was going to try to feed Patsy some crackers to see if she could swallow them. They sat her up in bed and the doctor asked Patsy to open her mouth. It took him a few tries, but finally, she did.

I was overjoyed that she had taken a command and followed it.

Then the doctor said, "Patsy, I want you to eat this cracker and try to swallow it."

Patsy looked a little puzzled, but after a few tries, she finally let the doctor put the cracker in her mouth.

I calmed my pounding heart so I could hear every crunch.

Patsy started to chew, and then chew a little more, and then chew a little more. I was so focused on waiting for her to swallow, that I was completely oblivious to everything else in the room. She was having some difficulty swallowing.

Under my breath, I was saying, "*Please God, make her swallow this,*" when, all of a sudden, she swallowed.

I wanted to see that again on instant replay. I started yelling and screaming and thanking God. It wasn't going to be years; it wasn't going to be months; it would be less than a week until she would be eating completely on her own with no feeding tube. Praise God!

I could finally see the light at the end of the tunnel, and it was a beautiful light to see. It is the same light that God talks about in His Word.

The light shines in the darkness,
and the darkness can never extinguish it.

(John 1: 5)

Reluctantly, I left Patsy at Shepherd, knowing that I could not see her for six long days. It was a good time for Linda to go home and recharge her batteries for a few weeks. Linda had done such a great job at Duke, watching every medicine and IV that went into Patsy's body and keeping Patsy comfortable and clean.

Her dedication and commitment far exceeded my expectations. I was going to miss Linda for those few weeks, but I knew she needed a break. For what was about to come, she would need all the rest she could get.

It was a long six days waiting to return to see Patsy. I would call Shepherd frequently to see how she was doing, and they would tell me that she was making a little bit of progress. Being the impatient man I am, though, I was hoping to hear that she was making progress by leaps and bounds. I just kept on praying.

It was Tuesday, March 7, and I was getting ready to visit Patsy. The six days had passed, and I had cleared my calendar for the whole day so I could spend it all with Patsy. I had been having dreams that Patsy was 100 percent healed, and I would just pick her up, take her home, and go back to the life we had before she was stricken with this monstrous disease.

I walked down the long hallways at Shepherd with butterflies in my stomach. It felt like puppy love. I couldn't wait to see her. As I walked into her room, Patsy was lying in bed resting. I went to her bedside and rubbed her cheek gently. She opened her eyes and gave me the biggest smile I had seen since her illness began. She seemed to recognize me and said, "Hi," along with some gibberish that sounded like Ron.

"Do you know who I am?" I asked.

Still smiling, she shook her head, "yes."

I gave her the biggest kiss on her forehead that I could drum up. I was jubilant. I had thought, at times, that she knew who I was, but now, without a shadow of a doubt, I was certain she knew me. I thanked God for this one step forward.

I spent the whole day with Patsy as she went through her different treatment therapies. The best part of this day was when she was walking. Although she was strapped to the therapist — to make sure she would not fall — she was powering her own movements.

Back in her room at the end of the day, I spent the whole evening talking to her about our kids and grandkids and catching her up on what she had missed while she was in her Rip Van Winkle sleep.

I didn't know how much she could absorb of what I was telling her, but it didn't matter. This was the first time I was alone with Patsy. My heart overflowed, even though I was holding a mostly one-sided conversation, with intervals of Patsy trying to say something, but unable to get the words out.

How much we take for granted! Sometimes, just having a simple conversation with the one you love can be exhilarating — especially when you haven't been able to communicate for a long time.

Another week went by, and Patsy was steadily improving. She was able to follow commands well, but not enough yet to have any independence. I was excited to see the progress. I wanted to thank God in a big way. I wanted everyone to know what He had done for Patsy and me.

I finally thought of a huge way to honor and glorify God and witness to His Word. I decided that a billboard proclaiming that Jesus had healed my wife would be the ultimate way. On it, I would refer to Psalm 91: 14-16... the verse that had sustained me through my most troubled times.

I told my associate pastor, Don, what I planned to do. A very godly man who knew the Bible inside and out, he asked me, "Ron, are you sure you want to do this right now?"

"Yes, I am," I responded. "Jesus will complete His promise. If I truly believe, then I must act without doubt or hesitation."

His response was, "If you believe it that strongly, then do it."

I ordered the first billboard. It would take several weeks to design the billboard and make up the sign and another couple of weeks to get it installed. I paid for it upfront — the cost of the design, the fabrication, and the first two months' rent.

I can say honestly that I never questioned whether I should have waited longer. In fact, one month later I put up another billboard. By the end of the year, I had nine billboards scattered all around the state of Georgia. On some, of the signs, I varied the verse, but all of them proclaimed that Jesus had healed my wife.

One of Ron's Nine Billboards

Another week had gone by, and Patsy was taking off. She was progressing steadily every day. Patsy could talk better, follow commands better, and do more for herself without assistance. One day when I came to visit, I found her washing the windows inside the cafeteria. I was elated. I joined in helping her clean the windows.

Patsy would have to relearn everything: how to dress herself, comb her hair, clean house, wash clothes, exercise, and pay bills. She would have to relearn her ABC's, every word in the English language, her numbers, math skills, how to drive. Driving... oh, we're not there yet. That's another story by itself.

Patsy's brain had been wiped clean by this vicious illness like a computer wiped clean by a computer crash. But sometimes, what the computer has lost is not totally gone — just misplaced. Then it can sometimes be retrieved using a

143

different route. Patsy's formidable job, with God's help, would be to build new pathways in her brain.

A few days later, I came to visit Patsy again. When I looked for her in all her usual therapy areas, I could not find her. I asked at the nurses' station, and they told me she'd had a setback and was in her room. I asked what kind of setback, and the nurse told me I would have to talk to Patsy's doctor. I rushed to Patsy's room. She was lying in bed. She didn't even recognize me. Patsy was almost like she had been when she first arrived.

At first, I freaked out. Then I tried asking Patsy questions, but she could not respond. I asked her to follow commands, but she couldn't understand. What was going on here?

I left the room to find Dr. Kaelin but was told he was not at the clinic today. The nurse referred me to the doctor on staff, and I went to his office. He told me that he had given Patsy a new medication which often helps enhance cognition. The medication had caused an extreme reaction, resulting in her regression. I asked him, what that meant.

"Well," he began, "we hope that, after the medicine has passed through her system, she will start to come back."

"What do you mean you hope?"

"We've never seen anyone have this kind of reaction," he replied. "So we don't know what to expect."

I had to use every ounce of my strength not to start yelling at this guy. What came to my head first was, "Lord don't let me judge by my eyes."

My anger started to subside, and I could begin to think rationally. I knew they were trying to do their very best for Patsy, and I needed to trust God. I had to remember that no one can get in the way of God's plan — no doctor, no medicine, no obstacle of any kind can stop the will of the Lord.

Again, I reached out to my friends and my church to explain what had happened. I asked them to pray for Patsy. By this time I knew the power of prayer and had seen the results.

I went back to Patsy's room and stayed with her for the rest of the day and into the night. Patsy stayed very quiet with no sign that she recognized me. It was like being back at Duke. I knew God would heal her, I just had to trust. I prayed at intervals all day and into the night. My faith was being tested, and I was barely holding on by a shoestring.

The next morning I got up very early. I wanted to get to Shepherd before the traffic built up. I was hoping and praying the medication would have passed through Patsy's system and she would have recovered all the progress she had made. When I got to Patsy's room, however, I could see at first glance that not much had changed.

I stayed with her the whole day, and I could start to see small improvements. She was more alert and made several unsuccessful attempts to talk to me. Even though it had been turned back to gibberish, her willingness to talk gave me hope.

It took 48 hours for the medication to completely clear out of Patsy's system. Then she began to catch up rapidly. After a few days, she was back to where she had been before the setback. Her progress was enough that the doctors were going to let me take Patsy to lunch and spend a whole four hours outside the facility.

Linda had just gotten back, and she would join us for this outing. I was so excited! I was going on a date with my girl. So what if we had a chaperone? I couldn't think of a better one than Linda.

I am a very persistent person, and I always want to do everything I can to fix things. When it comes to the people I love, I can be like a man on a mission. Some of my nicknames from the past are *Rocket Ronnie, Ram Rod Ronnie, Get 'er Done Ronnie*, and, of course, *The Fixer*. Now, you might wonder why I am telling you this. Read on.

Patsy, Linda, and I went to Houston's in Buckhead for lunch. The doctors and nurses had told me that her nutrition was very important… the greener the vegetable the better. We were about to order lunch, and I, aka *The Fixer*, ordered Patsy a healthy salad with grilled chicken. Linda ordered a prime rib sandwich, and I ordered the same. If you've never had Houston's prime rib sandwich, put it on your bucket list.

When the food was brought to the table, I could see by the look on Patsy's face that she didn't want the salad. She wanted Linda's sandwich. I tried to explain how important her diet was to her recovery, but she wanted no part of that salad, and she let me know it with a big scream. When I tried to reason with her, she began to yell at me in her gibberish speech.

Now Patsy may have lost her power of speech, but she hadn't lost her stubborn streak. And I could hardly blame her after being fed through a tube for so long. I backed off before it turned into an embarrassing scene, and, of course, Momma Grizzly gave her sandwich to her cub.

"Linda," I said, "I know you love this sandwich. You take mine."

I ended up with Patsy's salad. So, unfortunately, I was the one to get the good nutrition that day. I have had to learn to choose my battles. The salad battle was definitely a bad choice.

After lunch, we went for a ride in the downtown area. I wanted Patsy to get stimulation from outside the clinic to broaden her thinking with a variety of experiences. As we were driving around, Patsy was looking all around at people, cars, and buildings when she saw a dog. I could see the dog excited her. I thought of an idea. Billy the Kid was trained as a service dog. He could help comfort her and help her focus.

Tomorrow I would bring Billy-the-Kid to visit her at Shepherd. Fortunately, Shepherd approved of the experiment, and I was able to get permission.

Billy Comes for a Visit

The next day was Sunday, and I brought Billy in. I hadn't been able to spend much time with him lately. He had been passed around among trusted friends. They unanimously agreed that he was a joy. Although Billy was excited, his demeanor was serene, his actions were totally under control... and he was still only nine months old.

We arrived at the Shepherd court-yard, where Patsy and Linda were already sitting. When Patsy saw Billy and

Billy saw Patsy, the connection was instantaneous. They bonded immediately. I was convinced that Patsy had recognized him by the way she was smiling and reaching for him.

Patsy started to rub Billy's head, and Billy rested his head on Patsy's lap. Billy was just looking at Patsy and Patsy was looking right back at Billy. I saw a glimpse of the Patsy that I knew before her illness. She just glowed with joy having Billy's head on her lap... almost like a mother's joy for her little boy.

We will never really know for sure whether or not she recognized him. Patsy doesn't remember anything about her stay at Duke, Shepherd, or Shepherd Pathways. It would take months before all the lights were back on, and she could recognize everyone close to her.

Patsy was starting to regain more of her abilities. The clinic thought it would be good if we took Patsy home for the day. So the following Saturday, Patsy would come home for an eight-hour visit. If that went well, she would be released the following week. Then she could continue her recovery as an outpatient at Shepherd Pathways.

Linda and I picked Patsy up from Shepherd and drove to our house. As we walked in, Patsy noticed something on the coffee table that was out of place. Without hesitation, she moved it back to the right place. That response brought me great hope. She spent the whole day at home until it was time to go back to Shepherd.

Patsy seemed to marvel at everything she saw in the house. She could not speak well, but you could see by her facial expressions that she was enjoying herself. It seemed to me that Patsy knew where she was... that she was home. I now knew that she would definitely be coming home next week.

Tuesday, March 28, was a big, red-letter day. Patsy was being released from Shepherd Center. She would now get to start at Shepherd Pathways as an outpatient attending five days a week. We had gathered all the cards, flowers, novelties, and gifts that so many people had given Patsy at Duke and Shepherd. I looked at the drawings from the grandkids telling her, "Nana, get well soon and come home." They were getting their wish.

All the staff lined up along the hallway leading to the outside exit. They were so overjoyed that one of their patients was going home on a good note. Their efforts had made a difference with God's help. They were all hoping that Patsy would make a full recovery.

That day is a day I will never forget. Patsy had gone into Shepherd on a gurney, but, by the grace of God, Patsy walked out of Shepherd under her own power... no gurney... no wheelchair... no walker... no cane. I was feeling ten feet tall watching Patsy walk out of the hospital completely on her own. That was nothing less than miraculous! God's promise was becoming a reality. I knew I just needed to keep trusting and believing. Thank You, Jesus!

CHAPTER 11

The Road to Victory — When Will It Come?

It was Wednesday, March 29. Patsy had been home for less than 24 hours. Shepherd had given us a lot of instructions to follow. One critical instruction was that Patsy must not be left alone. If she had to get up and go to the bathroom, I was to get up and go with her.

"What if she gets up in the middle of the night, and I don't wake up?" I thought for a minute; then I had an idea. *"I will take the belt from my robe and tie it to a belt from another robe. I will tie one end around Patsy's waist and the other end around mine. That way, if she wakes up and forgets to wake me, she can't go far without me."*

It was the middle of the night, and I started to feel a tugging at my waist. I woke up immediately. It was Patsy, standing alongside the bed, trying to walk and going nowhere. But how could she move? She was anchored to a whale! I was glad my ingenuity had paid off. We were joined at the hips and stayed like that every night for months.

Linda had her job cut out for her too. Shepherd had told us three important things that were vital for Patsy's recovery. First, she was not supposed to watch a lot of television. Second, we needed to keep her stimulated by walking and talking with her. Finally, and most important of all, we could give her only one command at a time.

Linda would say, "Okay, Patsy, we are going to take a shower."

She would help Patsy get ready to take a shower. Once Patsy was in the shower, she would give Patsy another command. "Patsy, we are going to wash your hair."

Once that was done, Linda would give another command. "Patsy, now we are going to wash your body." Once Patsy was out of the shower, Linda would carefully give one command at a time so as not to confuse or frustrate her.

One morning, Linda was in the shower with Patsy, and she gave Patsy a second command too close to the first. Patsy was so frustrated that she pushed Linda against the shower wall. Patsy had never been a violent person, and this action was a complete surprise. What was going on?

It's all about brain connections. The brain is structured so that most information coming in from your senses goes first to the limbic system, the primitive part of the brain ruled by emotion. There, all the messages get sorted and sent to the right places in the higher-level cortex, the "thinking" part of the brain. Messages zoom around the cortex. One area makes sense of what your eyes are seeing. Another decides which foot to lift next when walking. This allows us to read books or run marathons.

But there's a glitch. When the limbic system receives a very emotionally charged message, it reacts immediately — it acts without thinking. It's like touching a hot stove. You don't have time to think about it and decide what to do before yanking your hand away. You just do it.

Limbic system reactions can be very fast. The information that Patsy was frustrated should have been sent to the cortex, where she could decide how to react. But, Patsy's illness had wiped out many of the connections in her "thinking" brain, which would have to be rebuilt. In the meantime, responses to strong emotions would often be out of her rational control. This would account for many of Patsy's problems in the months ahead.

When Linda told me about the incident, I sat down with Patsy like a father talking to his child, rather than a husband talking to his wife. Because her comprehension was so limited, we had to treat Patsy like a small child… a very hard thing for a husband to do. I had to explain to her that she could have hurt Linda or herself. This Patsy was completely different from the sweet, loving, caring Patsy that we both knew.

One morning after Linda had helped her get ready for the day, Patsy was lying on the bed watching TV. I knew I needed to get her to go walking with me.

"Patsy, let's go walking," I said.

She said, "No!"

"Patsy, we need to walk," I insisted. "It's important."

Patsy again refused. I paused and thought back to the "battle of the salad." That was a battle not worth fighting, and I gave it up. But this was an important issue, like the time when I wanted Patsy to go to Duke and get checked out. I was prepared to dig in and hold my ground. It was that important.

So I said, "Patsy you are going to walk if I have to pick you up and carry you outside."

Well, that's exactly what I had to do, with Patsy kicking and screaming all the way. It took a while, but she finally calmed down, and we started walking.

After a bit, Patsy saw two neighbors walking toward us.

"Don't talk," she urged in gibberish. "Keep going."

"Patsy, I can't be rude. I need to say hello."

I stopped to chat, whereas Patsy would not say one word to them. That was the complete opposite of her nature.

From the time I first met Patsy, she had always been a warm, bubbly, friendly person. But today, when asked how she was doing, Patsy wanted no part of any conversation. She turned away like a child that couldn't have her way.

"I am sorry," I said, a little embarrassed, hoping they would understand. "Patsy is tired and is not having a good day." Some days were like that.

Patsy was now going to school five days a week, and she hated it. I had hired an employee's wife named Ann, a helpful, caring woman, as a driver for Patsy's car. This left Linda free to stay in the back seat with Patsy and keep a close eye on her. And thank God I did. It always seemed that God was directing me on how to keep Patsy from harm's way.

One morning, Patsy pitched a fit. She didn't want to go to school. While the car was driving down the road, Patsy decided she was not going to school that day. So Patsy tried to exit the car while the car was riding on the freeway. Thank God we had child-locks, and thank God we used them. Patsy was desperately trying to get out of the car. When she failed to open the door, she started to take off all her clothes.

Poor Linda! She was battling with Patsy like a momma grizzly would fight with her cub to keep it out of danger. Linda's determination, her strength, and her unwillingness to give up finally calmed Patsy down. Linda was truly God sent. Linda and the child locks avoided a near catastrophe. Thank you, Linda, and thank you, Jesus!!!

Linda had a lot of stressful times managing Patsy's behavior while trying to re-teach Patsy everything that all of us take for granted: how to brush her teeth, how to comb her hair, how to cut her meat with a steak knife, even how to go to the bathroom properly.

Linda was unbelievably tough when she needed to be. She was also patient, kind, and loving. All her instincts were spot on. Linda knew how to anticipate potential issues before Patsy even faced them. It was as though she was born to do this job... a job that nothing could prepare you for... nothing, except God.

From time to time, Linda received help from an unexpected source... Billy-the-Kid. Billy seemed to be able to sense Patsy's frustration at times and had a remarkable ability to calm her stormy moods.

Billy – Patsy's Caregiver and Guardian

Billy would sit next to her as if to protect her from herself. He would often lay his head in Patsy's lap and gaze at her, especially when he sensed her frustration. With his gentleness and his loving nature, he seemed to be trying to console her.

Billy had been trained as a veteran service dog, but towards the end of his training, they discovered that Billy would spook at loud noises like gunshots or fireworks. Their loss was our good fortune. Billy was one of a kind. He would follow Patsy around the house right by her side as though he were making sure she didn't fall or do something dangerous.

We kept a baby video monitor in our bedroom, so, when Patsy was upstairs by herself, Linda or I could keep an eye on her. Using the monitor, I could see Billy-the-Kid lying on the floor right next to Patsy while she napped. It gave me a measure of peace.

Billy was amazing. Several years later, when he was full grown, I took him to downtown Woodstock, Georgia, on the Fourth of July. There was a big celebration with a parade and a lot of festivities... and I had forgotten Billy's leash. Instead of going back and getting it, I decided to let him walk off-leash. Billy stayed right by my side the whole time. It was wall to wall people. You could barely walk through the streets. Even with all the dogs, horses, cats, and a park loaded with squirrels, Billy never left my side.

And now, having Billy around took some of the burden off Linda. Although she could anticipate a lot of

Patsy's needs, she could not always anticipate Patsy's outbursts.

Patsy was having major outbursts of anger at school. One day, I received a call from the head psychiatrist at Shepherd Pathways. He asked me if I would come in to speak with him. They were having issues with Patsy's anger and behavior.

I felt like a parent being called to the principal's office because my child was misbehaving. I jumped into my car and proceeded to Pathways. My awareness of what was coming made the drive seem all too short.

Once I reached the parking lot at Shepherd Pathways, I started praying for wisdom, strength, and a solution to get Patsy on the right road. I knew God was going to heal Patsy. I just needed to understand what He wanted me to do. During this time, I felt that I was being tested beyond my measure.

But, God will never give you more than you can handle. I am living proof of that. If you keep Him first in everything, He will never forsake you. I believe that, when God said to put no other gods before Him, He was doing that for our own good. When you put God first before all others — religion, money, job, or anything else that you care about... there is nothing you can't overcome, nothing. He will be there with you every step of the way.

I walked into the clinic, not knowing what to expect or how I was going to deal with it. After I sat down, the doctor said, "Your wife has been acting out on a regular basis. She is belligerent and hateful and refuses to cooperate with the staff. I'm sorry to have to tell you this, but if Patsy continues to have these outbursts, she will not be able to continue here at Shepherd Pathways."

I sat there, stunned. I had the eerie feeling that I had entered the *Twilight Zone*. Nothing seemed real. This was not the way it was supposed to be.

My thoughts were interrupted when the doctor said, "Patsy is lying on the couch, and refuses to get up. Linda is there, trying to talk with her."

I nodded and got up slowly. I knew that Patsy needed to be in this school, and the stakes were high. I needed the wisdom of God to be able to reason with my wife in her angry, childlike state. I would need God to speak using my voice. As I walked down the long hallway to the room where Patsy was, I fervently beseeched Him to give me the perfect words.

As I walked into the room, I could see by her angry face how upset Patsy was. Glancing at Linda, I saw the look of despair on her face. I sat down with Linda beside me and asked Patsy what was wrong. She replied in half gibberish speech that she did not want to go to school. I felt as though I had gone back twenty years in time and was talking with my daughters about how important school was.

I knew this wasn't the real Patsy. How was I to get through to her? How could I reason with her so she would understand how important school was for her recovery? Again, I asked God to give me the perfect words. And He did.

"Patsy, do you know who I am?" I asked. She nodded yes.

"Do you know who Linda is?" She nodded her head again.

"Do you want to get better?" She nodded her head a third time.

"How do you think you can get better?" She just looked at me.

"That's right," I said. "You can't unless you attend this school and listen to your teachers and to Linda."

I told her how much I loved her, and then, for the first time, I told her what God had said to me – that she was going to be healed... totally healed. Then I said, "You have to do your part for this to happen. God expects that from you."

It was God's perfect words that finally reached her. She started to cry. I just wrapped my arms around her and started hugging her. It was one of those pivotal moments.

That day, Patsy made a major breakthrough in understanding that God was in this. I have to believe that

God was right there in the room when I was speaking to Patsy. The change in her disposition was dramatic.

From then on, Patsy began to cooperate at school and at home with Linda. She also started to fit in better, at school, and there were no more major incidents. My Patsy was starting to grow up.

CHAPTER 12

My Girl Was Growing Up!

It was now late spring. The weeks were flying by, and Patsy was continuing to make progress. One afternoon, I went to visit my beautiful wife for a lunch date at school. When I got there, I could see that she was interacting with people. She even introduced me to some of the patients she had met.

Most of them were in wheelchairs or wearing brain helmets to protect their skulls because parts of their skulls were missing. Some of those patients had their partial skulls surgically implanted inside their bodies. This was to preserve the skull until it was time to reattach it to the head.

Patsy was playing Florence Nightingale with the other patients. It was so good to see my darling wife reaching out to others as she used to. She was forming strong bonds with many people and especially with Linda. Patsy was finally trusting and relying on Linda without reservation. They soon became as inseparable as sisters. Later Linda and Patsy would refer to each other as wife-in-laws.

Linda was the one who made sure that Patsy received her medicine on time and in the correct dosage each day. Patsy was on a blood thinner for clots and another medicine to prevent seizures along with many others. At one point she was taking ten different medications several times a day. Linda made this challenging task look easy.

One of the major worries of trauma to the brain from infection is seizures. If Patsy were to have a seizure, she would never be able to drive again. And that included the new car I had bought her while she was in her coma.

I had purchased that car to demonstrate my faith in God's promise, and I believed that He approved and would protect Patsy. Sure enough, Patsy never had a single seizure... not then and not ever... by the grace of God.

Another of Linda's tasks was to coordinate Patsy's many doctor visits and schedule the blood work for monitoring the Coumadin she was taking. Blood monitoring was critical to assure that the Coumadin in her bloodstream was at the right level.

Linda also had to keep up with the constant changes in Patsy's school curriculum and make sure Patsy arrived at her sessions on time. Patsy was attending sessions of physical therapy, speech therapy, medical treatment, and hyperbaric therapy. In between, Linda was continually teaching Patsy about everything from soup to nuts.

One day, Patsy was at home and in her closet with Linda. You could have parked a bus in that closet. That's how big it was. It was filled with all Patsy's clothes and shoes, and I mean shoes. She had so many that she could have opened a shoe store.

Linda said to her, "This is all your stuff."

I think that day another light-bulb went on. Patsy said, "It is? It's all mine?"

Linda said, "Yep."

Patsy said, "I love it! I can't believe it's all mine."

There was a lot going on during this time. But Linda was able to find time to take Patsy to a variety of different stores to familiarize her with the routine of shopping. Linda's time management skills were incredible, just incredible. She could make any CEO stand up and take notice of her abilities.

One day, Linda and Patsy were going shopping. I told Linda to stop at the bank and pull out some cash. Linda took Patsy to the ATM and showed her how to use it. Patsy was excited at learning how to use a bank card.

Patsy asked Linda, "You mean I could get money out anytime?"

Linda laughed, "Only if you put money in first."

Patsy was learning about money, and beginning to understand the world a little better. When I heard the story that day, my heart was warmed. My girl... she was growing up.

Linda was such a trooper that she never complained, but I could see that the constant demands on her were wearing her down. I decided to take Patsy shopping for a day to give Linda a break and spend some time alone with Patsy.

I wanted to buy Patsy some gifts. I love to buy her gifts just to see the expression on her face. I asked Patsy what she wanted, and she told me she didn't really know. Now, guys, we all know that women never have enough shoes. So, despite the abundance of shoes in her closet, I figured we would go shoe shopping.

We went to store after store and looked and looked. Patsy wasn't enthusiastic about anything she saw. Finally, impatient as I am, I asked her, "How about these shoes. They look really nice," I said. "Try them on." So she did.

"Do you like them?" I asked

She looked at me and said, "Yes." So we bought them.

Later I found out that she was only shoe shopping to make me happy. She didn't really want to go, she didn't really want the shoes, she just wanted to go home. I had worn her out. *Rocket Ronnie* had used too much jet fuel that day. She told Linda I had totally exhausted her, but she thought that, if she said she liked the shoes, she could go home.

Back at Shepherd Pathways, Patsy was making major headway both in performing motor skills and following commands. She was becoming more independent, and her sparkling, effervescent self was returning. The staff was flabbergasted at her accomplishments.

It was now midsummer of 2006, and Patsy's progress was accelerating. I decided to throw her a big party. I invited family, friends, and church members to celebrate the fact that my wife was home. Like the father from the prodigal son story who wanted to give thanks, so did I.

I had the event catered and even hired a small band. It was a great day and evening. Even though Patsy did not yet look her healthy self, she thoroughly enjoyed it.

Linda, Patsy, and Amy at the Party

By this time, Patsy had learned to manage many of the everyday tasks of independent living. She could take care of her personal hygiene, sort and fold laundry, vacuum the floor, put things away in the right places, and use cooking utensils under supervision.

But, Patsy was still having difficulty with her gibberish speech. It was often hard to understand what she was trying to say. It was as though all the words in her mental filing cabinet had been dumped out in a heap, and the word Patsy was searching for was buried in the middle of the pile.

Linda was working harder than ever to improve Patsy's communication skills, but it was a slow process. Like putting together a gigantic jigsaw puzzle, Patsy's speech was being put back together slowly piece by piece. There were many pieces yet to go before the picture would be complete.

Patsy would have to learn to read written words and understand their meaning. She would need to quickly recall the right words to express her own thoughts out loud. Then she would need to be able to spell those words so that she could write them down. This was a daunting task.

Linda's commitment and determination were phenomenal. However, Patsy's long recovery was taking its toll on Linda. Linda's husband kept reassuring her that she could do it and that God expected her to finish the job. I realized that Linda was homesick, and came up with what I thought would be a solution.

I invited Linda's granddaughter, Katie, to come and stay with us for the rest of the summer thinking she would be good company for Linda. Katie was excited to come, and she was awesome!

Katie pitched right in and helped Patsy with math, phonics, reading, and writing. She had been blessed with the instincts and dedication of her grandmother, and I could sense the heavy weight beginning to lift from Linda's shoulders.

For some time, I had been thinking about taking Patsy on a trip to a place we had stayed before so that she could re-live some of her past experiences. The Breakers in Palm Beach had been one of our favorite places to go in Florida, and I hoped that returning there might trigger old memories. It also seemed like the perfect way for Linda to get a break and have some fun in the sun with Katie.

Before we left, Katie and Linda made flash cards with words and pictures to help spark Patsy's memory. They had many pictures of things that she would see along the way or at the beach.

Picture of Things Patsy Would See on the Trip, Made by Linda and Katie

Katie became a welcome addition to the Momma Grizzly family. She, too, was protecting Patsy and helping her to learn. This was a wonderful time for all of us. It did seem to spark Patsy memory. She began to use words related to the trip. We returned relaxed, refreshed, and ready to resume working on Patsy's recovery.

Patsy and Savanah with Billy in his Service Dog Uniform

We had all thought of the trip as a vacation from the hard work of Patsy's recovery. But, upon returning, it was evident to me that she had made improvement during the "vacation." So it was more than a vacation. It was like summer school and vacation all wrapped up in one.

The vacation had really paid off. Patsy was now a lot more aware of her surroundings and much more responsive during our interactions. Patsy's speech was still what I would call broken gibberish, but I was learning to understand her language... except, as you will see, when I was upstairs and she was downstairs.

CHAPTER 13

Patsy Takes the Wheel.

Prior to her illness, Patsy was notorious for her poor driving skills. Patsy had totaled three different vehicles from tailgating. She had difficulty parking the car in the garage. She had a tendency to hit the garage door, the garage door track, or the wall. I know because I paid for the repairs.

When we would travel by car, if Patsy was driving, she would tailgate on the freeway. You know better than to criticize your wife's driving skills. Patsy would say to me, "Ron, let me drive so you can get some rest." Her thought was noble, but, in reality, it made me so nervous that I couldn't relax and preferred to drive.

One Sunday morning in late August, we had returned home from church. We had planned to visit some friends. I wanted to change my clothes and was heading upstairs.

Patsy called up to me, "Ron, which car are we going to take?"

"The SUV," I answered.

"The little car is blocking the SUV," she hollered back.

"I'll move it when I come back down," I said.

She offered to go ahead and move the car for me. During this time, Patsy speech was often difficult to understanding including this time. I answered with, "Okay," figuring I would find out what she was asking when I got back downstairs. And I *would* find out.

When I finally returned downstairs, Patsy announced that she had gone ahead and parked the car in the garage.

"YOU WHAT?" I exclaimed. "YOU PARKED THE CAR IN THE GARAGE?" I envisioned my car customized for a demolition derby. I also feared that my garage door opener would no longer be a necessity.

I ran out to see how much damage was done. To my astonishment, Patsy had neatly pulled the car into the garage. It was centered, with the garage door shut. Everything was completely intact, and nothing was damaged! I was doubly amazed because it was a one car garage –very tight and not easy to pull into.

In the past, I had always insisted on pulling the car in myself. But Patsy had done it! She had parked the car perfectly! I never thought God was going to fix her driving skills too.

While we are on the topic of the extra benefits from God's healing, Patsy's bouts with extreme migraines were completely gone. Patsy hasn't had a single migraine in ten years. Thank You, Jesus.

It was now mid-September and time to pay a visit to Patsy's doctor. The doctor told us that Patsy could be weaned off *all* her meds. The trumpets were sounding... no more blood thinners, seizure medicine, cognition enhancers, or any of the other seven meds she was prescribed! These medicines are usually taken for a lifetime, and the doctors had thought for sure that this would be the case for Patsy. But God saw it differently. She was now med-free. Dr. Carlton commented to Linda that Patsy was "truly a miracle."

Thank You, Jesus!

Patsy's birthday was coming up. I wanted to take her to dinner, but not to just any old place. This was to be the dinner we had missed back on Valentine's Day... at a place where the waiter's name would be unpronounceable and the check would be astronomical. I had found just the place. I wanted this birthday to be extra special... intimate and romantic with just the two of us.

In the past, I had arranged surprise birthday parties for Patsy, but they were always big gatherings with lots of friends and family. The first one was when Patsy turned forty. I was going to have the party at our house, a few days before her actual birthday so she wouldn't be suspicious. I had to get her out of the house so I could make preparations.

I came up with what I thought was a clever plan. Patsy always loved to shop. She was every retailer's dream – the shopper who would "shop 'til she dropped." I had my assistant call her and ask if Patsy would like to go shopping at the outlet mall. I was sure she would go.

Unfortunately, I was wrong! She didn't want to go. I couldn't believe it. Now I was in panic mode. The caterers and decorators were scheduled to arrive very shortly. I had to think fast. The only thing I could think of, without tipping her off, was to start an argument. So I did, and she took the bait – lock, stock, and barrel. She stormed out of the house and went to join my assistant. She shopped alright that day, and I mean SHOPPED! I didn't know how much shopping she had done until I saw the credit card bill at the end of the month.

When we were first married, I would frequently go out of town golfing with my buddies. Every time I would go, Patsy would go shopping with a vengeance. It was her way of saying, "Knock it off, Ronnie. You're married now. How about saving some time for your wife?"

I finally got the hint when I saw the credit card charges. So I had no other choice but to decrease the golf trips with my friends to avoid going to the poor house. Patsy can sometimes be very effective at getting her point across without saying a word.

Anyhow, for the party, I had arranged that all the guests would park at a nearby church, and I arranged to have everyone shuttled from there over to the house. That way Patsy would have no clue when she pulled into the driveway. When she did arrive home that evening, she pulled up close to the house and pressed the garage door opener. When the door opened, to her surprise, waiting for her were seventy-five people who all yelled at once, "SURPRISE!"

Patsy was totally shocked. She started crying. Patsy got out of her car sobbing while everyone started coming up to her with hugs and wishing her a happy birthday. For me, the joy of watching that parade of people coming up to Patsy was priceless. She finally turned to me, wiping her tears and directing her big beautiful smile at me and said, "You got me, Ron!"

I love surprising Patsy, and this birthday would be no exception. I went out and bought her a very expensive, elegant evening dress and had it wrapped. I came home and sneaked into the house with the gift. I placed it under the coffee table and asked Patsy to come downstairs.

When she walked into the room, I was sitting on the couch. "Come sit down, Patsy. I want to talk with you."

As she sat down, her foot hit the gift box. She looked down and asked, "What's this?"

"What's what?" I replied.

"This box under the table," she answered in her half-gibberish speech.

I said, "You mean the box that's wrapped like a gift under the table?"

"Yes," she answered.

"I wonder what it is. I guess you'll have to open it to find out." I replied.

Patsy grabbed the box and noticed an envelope on top. She handed it to me and asked me to read it to her.

"It says, To My Queen from Your White Knight."

"Oh! For me? From you?" she exclaimed. "Can I open it now?"

"Yes," I replied. "It's an early birthday present. See what it is."

She began to tear off the paper like a little girl at Christmas. When she brushed away the tissue paper, her eyes opened wide like silver dollars."Oh, Ron, it's beautiful!" With a little twist of gibberish in her speech, she asked, "But WHERE will I be able to wear it?

"That's your next surprise, Patsy," I answered. "I'm taking you out for your birthday to a very special place for dinner. And you will need a dress like this to wear for appropriate attire."

Patsy looked at me with tears of happiness rolling down her cheeks and said, without any hesitation and as clear as a bell, "Ron, I LOVE you so much."

"LOVE!" That word set my heart pounding. It brought me back to our first date and the first time I ever heard her say that word. I had so longed to hear that word again from her lips and it finally came... My Patsy was coming back. I cherished this moment. It was the first time since Patsy's illness that we were able to have an intimate conversation where I wasn't doing most of the talking. And it was wonderful.

It was the night of Sept 18th, Patsy's birthday. I was so excited, and so was Patsy. This was our first formal dress-up date since last year, and I was in total euphoria. Patsy was getting ready, and our daughter Amy was helping Patsy with her makeup.

Amy yelled down the stairs to me, "She is ready, and she's coming down!"

My heart was full of anticipation as I waited at the bottom of the steps. There she was, as radiantly beautiful as I had ever seen her. Her gown fit her perfectly. The sequins on her dress made her blue eyes shine like the stars in the sky. It was a déjà vu moment that brought me back to the night of our nineteenth anniversary when she walked down the stairway of heaven. This time, I was thanking God for every step she took.

As Patsy and I started to leave, Amy said, "Don't be out late, y'all. You have a curfew."

"Don't wait up," I told her. "It's going to be a late night." And off we went as if we were off to the prom. It was to be an enchanted evening.

At the restaurant, the waiter's name actually was unpronounceable. Fortunately for Patsy, it made her partially incoherent speech less noticeable. I'm sure, most people butchered his name.

Patsy was studying the menu. As you know, Patsy was learning to read all over again. I could see that she was lost in the menu. In her gibberish speech, Patsy was trying to ask me questions about the different menu items. I was trying to answer her questions. However, I was having a hard time deciphering the foreign cuisine as well. It was like the blind leading the blind.

Finally, I asked Monsieur Unpronounceable for help. I said, "You pick our dinner for us. If you get it right, you will be amply rewarded." The dinner was over the top, and so was his tip.

For the first time in a long time, Patsy was giving me those goo-goo eyes, and I was loving it. Another light bulb had turned on. Patsy was finally remembering how much she loved me.

Patsy and I slow danced together that night. I thought back to the night we first met when I was almost too unsure of myself to ask her to dance. This time it was more than just a magical dance. It was a miraculous dance.

Having Patsy in my arms made me realize God's awesome power. Not long ago, the Star Wars machine completely engulfed her body. I could barely hold her hand. Now, my arms could completely encircle her as we swirled on the dance floor. It was surreal.

We were of one heart and one mind that evening. I didn't want the evening to end. But the restaurant was closing, so we started heading for home. We did make it home before our curfew and before our car turned into a pumpkin.

It was now late September, and I knew Patsy was going to have to pass her driving test. Once you have any type of brain injury, you have to retake the test. I was taking Patsy out for her first driving lesson on the road. She had been in a classroom course at Shepherd Pathways, but she had not been behind the wheel yet except for the garage incident. I was going to take her out to see what she could do.

We were in the garage, and Patsy had just started the car with some instructions from me. At that moment, two of our daughters and Linda came into the garage.

I asked the three of them, "Would anyone like to come with us?"

"No, No!" came the chorus.

"That's ok! We'll stay home."

"You take her out."

I could see by their faces they wanted no part of driving with Patsy. I think they were afraid for their lives and ours too! If you could have seen the expressions on their faces, you would have thought I was asking if they wanted an enema or something like that. Nevertheless, her first excursion behind the wheel was uneventful, and I found myself almost beginning to relax.

Patsy behind the Wheel

Patsy was more aware than ever of how important her participation was for her total healing. I believe there was a reason for the way God planned Patsy's healing. I believe her story demonstrates not only His power but the life lessons He wants to teach all of us. Through adversity comes joy when you believe.

When troubles come your way,
consider it an opportunity for great joy.
For you know that when your faith is tested,
your endurance has a chance to grow.
So let it grow,
for when your endurance is fully developed,
you will be perfect and complete,
needing nothing.

(James 1: 2-4)

CHAPTER 14

Patsy Joins the Fight - and God Is in Her Corner.

F all was arriving. It was late October, and the race was on for Patsy to get her driver's license before her new car arrived. She had less than thirty days! That car represented a major milestone in her recovery, and I was determined that Patsy, and no one else, was going to drive it home.

"Well," I thought. *"I can always pay for the car and let it sit until Patsy is ready to drive it home."*

And yet, something about that thought didn't sit right with me. I knew God's timing was always perfect. I had already seen it firsthand. Surely, it wasn't my place to tell God how to do His job. Still, I must say, the thought did cross my mind.

"No, Ronnie," I said to myself. *"You need to just trust Him. That's what you've been doing all along."*

Linda had been working feverishly to teach Patsy all the skills she would need for a completely independent life.

Linda focused on two different areas. One was to help Patsy regain her language skills – reading, writing and speaking. The other was to help Patsy to rebuild her memory of people and events from the past and the present. Linda's innovative teaching style seemed to be in perfect accord with Patsy's learning style. However, the task ahead was formidable.

Patsy would have to relearn all the words she had forgotten. Everything had a name – animals, household furnishings, countries, foods, people in the news, and especially the people in her life.

Using these words, she would have to build sentences so that she could talk intelligently to people. Linda would also have to teach Patsy the common social skills so that she would be comfortable interacting and talking with people.

Patsy had forgotten the letters of the alphabet. The names, along with the sounds, of letters had to be relearned before she could read and write. The most pressing need at this time was for Patsy to read well enough to pass her driver's test which was rapidly approaching.

Linda took every opportunity to probe Patsy's memory for what she could remember from the past and work to fill in the gaps. When Patsy first started on her long recovery she couldn't recognize any pictures of family members, much less remember their names.

Amy had helped by making cards showing pictures of relatives with their names on the back. Our daughter Lisa sent a framed picture box showing the grandkids. Linda used these to help Patsy relearn the names of all the people she used to know. She also worked on the names of our current friends and people from church.

Pictures of Relatives with Names on the Back, Made by Amy

Patsy would study these pictures and repeat the names over and over again trying to remember who they were. At first, she could remember only a few, and we would continue to remind her again and again.

Pictures of the Grandkids, from Lisa

Despite the frustration, Patsy would keep trying until she was exhausted. Patsy's stubbornness was now a benefit. She would not quit. Patsy knew God's promise and she was going to fulfill her part.

I remember witnessing another daily event. Linda and Patsy would watch the news together, and Linda would explain the events that were occurring as well as related events from the ten months when Patsy had been virtually absent from the real world. There was so much to learn.

Patsy was working very hard to overcome all the obstacles in front of her. I could only imagine the immense effort it took her to hurdle over the roadblocks set in front of her. I could see how determined she was to fully recover. Patsy was now more focused than ever on stepping up the healing process. Patsy is a fighter. With her boxing gloves on and God in her corner, my Patsy was going to knock out her disabilities one punch at a time.

Patsy's persistence slowly began to pay off, and Patsy began remembering names of people and some events of her distant past. Linda or I would tell her stories about our daughters or about one of those funny moments in our lives, Patsy would say, "Oh yeah."

She had a more difficult time with short-term memory of people and places from recent times. Linda was very creative in the methods she used to jog Patsy's memory, and Patsy responded well to Linda's approach.

On occasion, Linda would bring Patsy to my office to help trigger memories. My employees would interact with Patsy and share moments they had spent with her. I believe, for the first time, they didn't think they'd have to call the guys with the white suits and the nets. They were in awe. Nobody ever thought that Patsy would come walking through those doors, looking the way she did, let alone interacting with them.

I believe that some of my employees became closer to God through seeing His goodness and power. They realized that they had witnessed a miracle. Even though Patsy still had challenges ahead, the beauty was that she could overcome and learn from them.

Patsy would spend hours at the office even trying to do some of the work that she used to do. These visits helped her mentally and emotionally and strengthened her confidence. All of this played a part in the healing process.

I knew how far Patsy had come from the day she had entered Shepherd. But still, there were so many patients at Shepherd who were suffering from brain injuries and who were *not* recovering as Patsy had. I prayed for them often, and I would ask, "Why us, Lord? Why did you bestow this miracle on Patsy and me, but not on all the others who called your name?"

I had no idea why. I was truly grateful, but the question still perplexed me. The mystery was one I would continually try to understand.

We were into November now, and Patsy was still not ready for her driver's test. Patsy continued to work at her driving skills learning all the road signs and signals along with how to be a defensive driver. She knew that her new car was coming soon. Although she still struggled with some aspects of driving, she was determined to be ready. Within a few weeks, we expected a call from David saying that her car had arrived.

David called from the dealership sooner than expected. He said, "I need to apologize to you. Patsy's car will not be delivered until late December. I am so sorry for the delay."

"*This guy's apologizing,*" I thought to myself, "*and I am elated.*" God had intervened for me again.

He started to explain that there was so much demand for the new model change that the factories were behind. Now, keep in mind, David did not know anything about what had happened to Patsy.

"David that's great!" I exclaimed.

David must have thought at this point, "*Either this guy is the most understanding customer in the world, or he is missing a few nuts and bolts.*"

But all he said was, "Wow! Most customers would have a cow!"

"David," I said, "I must tell you something. When I ordered this car for Patsy back in January, she was in a coma at Duke Hospital in Raleigh... on life support."

"You have to be kidding me! Do you want me to cancel the order?"

"Absolutely not, but the delay is good."

"What do you mean the delay is good?"

"Patsy is very close to getting her driver's license back, and I think the end of December will be the perfect time for Patsy to have her license and pick up the car.

"She has to take her driver's test again?" he asked.

"Yes," I answered. "Anytime you have a major brain injury, you have to get a clearance from a doctor and retake the driver's exam."

"Wow!" he said. "It must have been pretty serious."

I told him it was, but that God had taken the S out of serious and put the G into grace when he healed Patsy.

After a moment of silence, he told me that he would put a big bow on top of the car and make a big deal out of it when Patsy came to pick up the car.

"Great!" I said. "Let me know when it comes in." I knew for sure now that God would time it perfectly.

Patsy was at a point where all Linda's pushing and pulling and coaxing and encouraging was paying off. Linda was not needed as critically as she had been before.

Patsy had become steadily more self-sufficient. Her goal was to be completely independent. Her desire for independence was the force that drove her to continue to learn. She no longer needed the micromanaging and one-on-one teaching that Linda had so painstakingly provided.

The job God had assigned Linda to do was nearly complete. It was time for an exit strategy so Linda could go home.

Patsy and I started to talk about what we could do to show Linda and Jerry, in a big way, how much we appreciated all the sacrifices they had made. It was nearly Thanksgiving, and it suddenly hit me — the perfect gift.

CHAPTER 15

With His Grace Comes His Promise.

Patsy was well on her way back to a normal life. "*We are a team again,*" I thought, "*and we are ready to do God's work together once more.*" So I began putting my plan into action.

Patsy and I had founded a ministry called *The Nite of Hope Atlanta*. Each year, we provided an elegant, fine-dining Thanksgiving dinner for the many homeless families in Atlanta. Last year in 2005, we had served one thousand homeless people and their families at the World Congress Center Ballroom, the same ballroom where President George W. Bush had held a fundraiser a few years back.

All the guests received a seven-course dinner, along with the gift of God's love from all the volunteers. And every man, woman, and child went home with a brand-new winter jacket. The inscription embroidered on the jacket said: JESUS CARES.

Nite of Hope – 2005

This year we wanted to do even more to let everyone know about the special thanks we felt for Patsy's amazing recovery. We wanted to show how loving and caring God is and to demonstrate His love in a mighty way.

The only way we can show God's love here on earth is by loving and caring for each other, one human being at a time. God calls upon us to love our neighbor. For Linda, giving and caring seemed to be simply a part of her nature. What could be a more fitting tribute to Linda than to give her a major part in this grand occasion of giving?

This year we would also double last year's numbers and have two thousand homeless families at the World Congress Center. There they would share in our celebration of gratitude. We would need five hundred volunteers — some to serve dinner while others sat with the families at their tables, sharing fellowship and God's Word.

We arranged a program for them that would give any New York Broadway show a run for its money. There were singers, dancers, and theatrical performances. The music included Christian rappers, gospel singers, and instrumental solo performances. The MC was masterful in his speaking. And, once again, every man, woman, and child went home with a brand-new winter jacket embroidered with "JESUS CARES."

Nite of Hope – 2006

Of course, no great Thanksgiving would be complete without a pre-visit from Santa and his entourage to see who was being naughty or nice. So we invited Santa and Mrs. Claus along with one of their helpers, an elf. Guess who those three might be? You got it — Patsy, Linda, and me.

It didn't take much to turn my over-nourished body into a deep-voiced Santa. But Patsy had a bigger challenge. By this time, she was starting to look like her beautiful young self again. So now we needed to transform Patsy into an older woman so she would look the part.

I thought back to the guy at Shepherd who had asked if I was wheeling my mother in. I'd love to hear what he'd have to say now.

We all dressed up for our debut as Santa, Mrs. Claus, and the Number One Elf to really look the part and to give all those children the Christmas experience that you and I take for granted. We had the complete attention of the children in the ballroom that night — a night, I believe, those kids won't ever forget.

That night was wonderful. Patsy was so vibrant and filled with love and joy. She was glad to be able to serve God in a way that would have been impossible just a few months earlier.

I will never forget that evening. Patsy was back, and we were serving God together again. You could see the glow in my heart shine right through my Santa suit. My feet never touched the ground as I floated on a cloud of euphoria.

On the way home, I was thinking of another perfect gift to show our appreciation for the sacrifices both Linda and Jerry had made. I've always been very spontaneous — a kinder word than impulsive – especially when it comes to vacations. I am sure my ADHD played a role in my spontaneity.

Patsy would tell me that she loved the spontaneous part of me. I would often surprise her with a birthday party, or maybe a gift for no special reason. I might also come home and say, "Pack up and grab the kids. We're going on a trip!"

One time, my daughter Julie came over to my house with her husband. She was crying and very upset because she was having a rough time at work and wanted some consolation from her dad. Being *Mr. Fixer,* I had an idea.

"To me, this sounds like a road trip to Florida. Don't you think so, Julie?"

"Wow! Do you mean it, Dad? Right now?"

"Of course I mean it. Go home and pack and we'll head off to anywhere."

I love to do things without planning. It feels more like an adventure that way. I picked them up, and we headed south, not knowing where we were going or where we would stop that night.

Now, I would use that spontaneity to show my appreciation to Linda and Jerry. A road trip... sorta. But this time, I had a specific destination in mind.

I asked Linda, "Have you ever been to New York City during Thanksgiving?"

She said, "No."

"Have you ever been to New York City?"

Again she said, "No."

"Call Jerry," I said. "We're all going to New York City to see the Christmas lights and the decorations... and, not only that... the Christmas special at Radio City with the Rockettes, live with Santa."

"Are you kidding me?"

With mock seriousness, I answered, "I would kid about some things, but I would never kid about a trip."

Two days later, Patsy, Linda, Jerry, and *Rocket Ronnie* were on a plane heading for The Big Apple. It was going to be a memorable trip and a fitting thank-you for Linda's long service to Patsy and Jerry's solo upkeep of the farm.

Ron, Patsy, Linda, and Jerry in a Horse-Drawn Carriage in New York City

We had so much fun in New York City. Patsy loved it. She marveled at all the tall buildings and the hustle and bustle of the people who lived there. When we went to see the Rockettes, they were off the hook. It was a Christmas wonderland event.

All the decorations and lights for Christmas were magical making the trip very special. I must say, Rockefeller Center looks bigger on TV, but in person, it was intimate and enchanting.

We stayed right across the street from Central Park. When you walked outside, it smelled like you were on a farm... like horse manure. The prices in New York City are very high, but I guess there was no extra charge for the authentic country aroma.

All the great foods, the street vendors, and the people performing on the streets created a time to remember. It was different from anywhere else we had ever been. Patsy and Linda were captivated. I think we all wanted to stay longer, but we knew that we needed to get back.

We arrived back in Atlanta still feeling the enchantment of all the sights and sounds of New York City. But, it was time to get back to the mission at hand.

Patsy was nearly ready to take her driving test. She had worked very hard to get her driving skills back in the past few months. I can tell you, they were back, and better than they were before her illness. God had given Patsy something extra along with her healing. He had cured her of tailgating and turned her into a defensive driver as well. I never again had to tell Patsy she was following too closely or driving too fast. It was amazing, just amazing! Patsy's negative driving habits were simply gone.

One time, John Pruitt on Channel 2 ABC Action News interviewed Patsy for a Christmas special called *Small Miracles*. She told him that she could drive better now than she had before she got sick. I think John was taken aback by Patsy's comment. For a few seconds, he was speechless... then all he could think to say was, "Really?"

It was December 21, 2006. Linda was to head home for good later that day. But, like all momma grizzlies, she had to make sure her young cub could fend for herself. Linda's commitment was like no other. There is no doubt in my mind that Linda's presence was an instance of divine intervention. Only God could have arranged things so perfectly.

I will never forget what Linda did for Patsy and my family. Linda is a true certified angel who has earned her wings twice over. Clarence, from the movie "It's a Wonderful Life," would be smiling and clapping for her.

The day had finally come for Patsy to take her driving test. She had worked hard to be ready for this test, and I can tell you, she was ready. My only concern was that she might become overwhelmed if she felt pressured by the state official. Patsy's skills were new enough that stress could cause her to get flustered. I was praying, and so was Linda.

As we watched Patsy go through the test with the official, she looked pretty sure of herself. Linda and I were hanging onto each other as each command from the state official was given. Patsy responded beautifully. Linda and I were crying. My girl was doing it. God's promise seemed more evident than ever. I wanted to cheer as Patsy sailed through the final part of the test.

Patsy had done it!! She had passed the test! Praise the Lord. Thank you, Jesus.

I was so happy that day I could have flown Linda home to Houston on my back. It was that wonderful. It was as if your doctor had just pronounced you cancer-free. You were not going die; you were going to live a full and completely normal life.

We dropped Linda off at the airport. Saying goodbye was bittersweet. Linda had done her job with such love, care, and efficiency that she had become part of our everyday family. We were really going to miss her, but we knew it was time for Linda to go home. Linda had completed the astronomical task I had placed on her shoulders. Patsy was now well on her way to a full recovery.

My heart was full of joy and sadness because of the bond that I had formed with Linda. By her example, she had taught me a lot about commitment, sacrifice, and true compassion. We will never forget Linda. I can only hope that I can immortalize her in this book.

I was driving home with Patsy... both of us missing Linda... when the phone rang. You know what comes next, right? Yep! It was a call from David at the dealership.

"Ron, I am sorry it has taken so long to get your wife's car in, but they are unloading it off the truck right now. We will have the car ready, not tomorrow, but Saturday morning."

"David, don't be sorry. God's timing is always perfect. Patsy just passed her driving test a few hours ago. So Saturday morning is perfect!"

The two days could not come fast enough. Saturday arrived, cold and clear. Patsy and I had invited a friend along to take pictures of this memorable moment. He picked us up and drove us to the dealership.

As we pulled into the dealership, there it was — Patsy's car. The midnight blue car with a gigantic red bow on top jumped out at us. It was like seeing God's promise in 3D.

I had alerted David to our arrival time in advance, and he had all the employees outside waiting for us. Patsy said to me, "Why are all those people standing outside?"

I said, "Because they want to see God's miracle."

Patsy said, "Really?"

I said, "Patsy, all God's grace and His promise, along with all of your hard work, will inspire the people here today. They are witnessing a miracle." We got out of my friend's vehicle and walked over to Patsy's new car.

Patsy opened the car door. I could almost hear the voice of God again, this time saying, *"Your wife has been healed."* I couldn't hold back the tears that rolled down my face. I thought to myself, *"I wasn't a fool. I wasn't nuts. God did exactly what He said He would."*

**Pats
y in Her New Car with a Big Red Bow**

Now, the light at the end of the tunnel was clear, strong, and radiant. It shone so brightly that I could see the entire path of Patsy's recovery. All the pieces of the puzzle were joined together. I could finally have peace knowing that God had completed His promise.

The dealership made a big deal out of delivering Patsy's car. I could see the belief in the eyes of those present. The joy and the hope it gave to everyone there would flow into their own lives... to be remembered for a lifetime.

As we were about to leave, Patsy, being her usual generous self, said, "Ron, you can drive it home if you want."

"Patsy," I said, "the only person driving this car home is you. I've been waiting for this moment for almost a year."

I began to thank God over and over. His Word is real and it is the truth. And, that day, He had confirmed it. (Mark 11:24) *"I tell you, you can pray for anything and if you believe that you received it, it will be yours."*

Patsy and I got into the car and she started up the engine. The sound of the car was like God's rolling thunder assuring me that this is real. Patsy fastened her seatbelt and put the car into drive. With Patsy at the helm, we sailed into the sunset. I thought to myself, *"This is like a movie with a great ending... only it's real."* That's the best kind of movie.

God directed it by telling me
He was going to
heal Patsy.
He produced it by giving me
the grace to have
faith.
He edited it by changing
the course of Patsy's
illness.
And He distributed it by having me
write this book and having
you read it.

I now believe I know why God may have healed Patsy in the way He did. It was not just that He is a healing God and does answer our prayers. It is also because He wants us to glorify Him. When we glorify God, it is as though He has a mirror in heaven that reflects His glory back down to us.

His purpose is to give us faith, hope, and the knowledge that He is real and always within reach which benefits us. That's how awesome God is. He loves us that much and His love is that perfect.

God could have healed Patsy supernaturally in the blink of an eye when she was near death. He could have told Patsy to get up and walk, just as Jesus told Lazarus to come out. There would have been a moment of awe as with so many other miracles that happen that way. But, like them, it would soon be forgotten except by the people who were helped.

Instead, I believe God wanted to use this book to keep alive the story... not just to show that he still performs miracles... but, more, to demonstrate how His grace can work in our daily lives when we persevere. I believe, through this story, He wants us to know that His grace and love are enough to give us the power of faith and trust... so we can do our part... when our part seems nearly impossible... if only we believe... even if no one else believes.

I have more peace and joy in my life now than I ever had with all the material riches I once owned. But joy comes only from the Lord when you trust Him. Joy is constant no matter if you are on the top of the mountain or down in the valley. Joy is the true wealth in our lives. It can't be printed, and no one can steal it, burn it, or destroy it unless you choose to allow it.

The story of Patsy's miracle contains many stories showing the power of faith and trust. They show how God can extend His grace to His purpose for our lives, to our marriages, our finances, our careers, our deficiencies, and our extended families...

If only we would ask...
If only we would listen...
If only we would trust...
If only we would believe...

EPILOGUE

Thoughts from Patsy

Hello, my name is Patsy Tripodo. This book tells about a piece of my life that I cannot remember at all. I read this book as Ron was writing it, one chapter at a time.

I finally learned my story and all the things that happened to me in that time, and I can truly appreciate how blessed I am. I am blessed to be alive and to be with my wonderful husband, Ron. I am blessed by the love of all the people who cared and prayed for me. I am blessed to be able to read this story and to write this message to you. Most of all, I am blessed to have God with me, so close in my heart.

I cannot remember much of the time right before my illness. I have no memory of the cruise. I do recall Ron putting Billy in my lap at the airport, but I don't remember the near accident at all. I have been told about putting eye makeup on my cheeks and going to Duke for all those tests, but I remember nothing.

It is sometimes hard to tell the difference between what I have been told and what I actually remember. But I do know for sure that I have no memory of anything at Duke, or Shepherd, or Shepherd Pathways or of all the doctors, nurses, and other people who worked so hard with me.

I wish I could go back to see every one of them, show them what they accomplished, and tell them how grateful I am. I wish I could personally thank everyone who prayed for me. But I can't, so the best I can do is to thank you all here.

The earliest memories from my recovery are of sitting at the kitchen table with Linda and Katie, learning from the flashcards they and Amy had made. I can also remember sitting in the family room with Ron, Linda, and Katie, having our morning coffee and listening to the news. But I don't remember much else from that time.

I had so much to relearn — how to talk, dress myself, do the laundry, fix a meal and on and on. At first, when I was getting better, I didn't think too much about anything else. I was content to live each day as it came. It was just so great to have my husband close to me and to be happy with him.

After a while, I wanted to be able to work with Ron in his business as I had done before. But, first, I had to learn to read, write, and do math. The more I learned, the more I realized how much I had forgotten. I went to the Huntington Learning Center to work with a tutor named Muriel. I had to start by learning the alphabet all over again! It took more than a year and a lot of very hard work. I was still going for bariatric treatments, and they would tire me out. Sometimes I just wanted to go to heaven and be with Jesus.

Back then, everything seemed so hard here on earth. But I did learn to read again, and I have never stopped reading. Now, I am so glad to be alive. I keep telling God, "Thank you, thank you, thank you for my life."

For Ron and me, the ten years after my illness were an uphill battle. But every year we grew closer and closer to each other. I have started working again with my tutor, Muriel, so I will be able to speak and write as well as I read. Watching Ron working such long hours every day on this book has made me want to work as hard as he does. I want my recovery to be complete so I can serve God as living proof of His love.

Now that it's over, I am not sorry about what happened to us because we are both closer to God than ever. I am only sorry for all the suffering it caused Ron. Until I read the book, I had no idea what he went through. But even that was necessary.

Ron had planned this book back in 2008, but he expected to have someone else write it as he did with the websites. It took all these years of trying and failing and trying again for him to be ready to write it himself with God's help.

I would never have believed that my husband wrote this book if I hadn't watched it happen. I know that God was with him the whole way. He couldn't have done it alone. My husband who never sat still, who never read a book, sat there writing for eight or nine hours at a time. The story just poured out. Then Muriel would come over and I'd see them with their heads together for hours working on grammar or hunting for the perfect word. It took just sixty-one days from start to finish.

I have been blessed to read Ron's book and to reflect on what happened and what my purpose is in all this. I believe God wants me to tell everybody about Him. I feel God so strongly in my own heart, and I want the same for everybody else. I love people, and I hope that by knowing me, they will feel God's presence in me and want to have God in their hearts too. I believe that is His purpose, and I know it is mine.

EDITOR'S NOTE

Thoughts from Muriel

I t feels strange to be writing an editor's note. I am not really an editor. I'm a teacher. First, I was Patsy's teacher and then Ron's. In 2008, Patsy came to the Huntington Learning Center in Woodstock, Georgia, where I worked with her as she relearned how to read and write. With her unique learning problems, I found the need to create many special materials, which I bound in a three-ring notebook labeled Patsy's Phonics Practice.

Patsy was making excellent progress in reading, and we were about to focus on writing and spelling when Ron's business crumbled. Patsy and Ron left for Florida, and I lost, not only a student, but a dear friend.

Sadly, I placed her notebook among the seldom-used materials on the top shelf in my office. Each year, when I cleared my cramped office of unneeded materials, I came upon Patsy's Phonics Practice. It was taking up much-needed space, and I could reuse the cover. I would take it down, start to toss the contents, and find I just couldn't. So back on the shelf it went, over and over again for five years.

Then one day, I got a call from Huntington telling me that someone named Ron Tripodo was trying to get in touch with me and wondered if I still worked there. I couldn't believe it! Patsy was back, and she wanted to resume her lessons.

This time we worked at her house. The first time, to Patsy's delight, I produced Patsy's Phonics Practice, preserved all those years from the trash bin. We were overjoyed to be working together again.

I found that Patsy had been reading constantly during those five years, and she had become an accomplished reader. What she needed now was to bring her speaking, writing, and spelling up to the level of her reading. It was during this process that I got to know Ron for the first time.

Ron was very interested in how I was teaching Patsy and wanted to know what he could do to help. After her lessons, they often asked me to stay for lunch, and I would explain to Ron what was going on in Patsy's brain, and what I was doing to help her rebuild what she had lost.

In one of our conversations, the subject of ADHD came up, and I explained to him the many symptoms, causes, and remedies I had learned about while raising my own ADHD daughter. Ron listened intently and wondered if he might have it. Now Ron is a walking billboard with ADHD written on it in monstrous, fluorescent letters. I managed not to burst out laughing and indicated as tactfully as I could that it was a definite possibility.

Over the weeks, he spent more and more time describing and asking about the symptoms he had experienced since childhood. And the lights began to go on. At that very time, Ron was planning a career change which would require a lot of reading and test taking. He wondered if some of the medications I had talked about might help him. I told him that it was definitely worth a try, but he would have to get an evaluation by a doctor first. I fought the urge to tie him up and drag him to the doctor's office.

No need! It didn't take long before he approached Dr. Early on his own, and you know the rest. I have worked with scores of ADHD children, and have seen a dramatic improvement in many after starting medication. The change in Ron blew me away. For the first time in his life, he sat down and actually began reading books. His impatience and restlessness were on a tether. He listened and thought before he spoke.

At that point, he realized that he was having a hard time comprehending what he read and asked if I could teach him to read better. Frankly, I was reluctant at first. I had no idea how to approach his type of problem. But he was set on the idea, and I thought it only fair to try.

The first thing I discovered was that Ron was starting with two of the most difficult books he could have picked. Having never been a reader, he was not familiar with complex sentence structure or archaic language. He would get lost in long strings of sometimes unfamiliar words. As he read a passage aloud, I would help him decipher it.

I found that, with proper medication, Ron is a fast learner. He is perceptive and insightful, and his memory is exceptional. His reading was improving steadily, and I was becoming quite optimistic. That was until he told me that he was going to write a book, and I was going to help him.

"Nooo!" I screamed silently. Then I said, "Ron, you aren't quite ready to write a book. You have to read books before you can write them. We've just begun looking at grammar, and your grammar is atrocious. You don't know how to write a paragraph. A book is made of paragraphs. You don't know what makes a complete sentence. Paragraphs are made of sentences. Why don't we work on grammar first while we improve your reading by exploring different kinds of books? You could be ready in a year or maybe less, but not now."

"Yeah, right!" Ron does have a stubborn streak.

On June 3, 2016, Ron emailed the first section of the book to me for editing. The grammar was atrocious, but the ideas were powerful and the language was expressive. I fixed the grammar, and the next day we put our heads together and smoothed it out. As I said before, Ron is a fast learner.

He studied my corrections and learned from them. Sometimes we edited together so that he could see why I made the changes that I did, and he learned. His writing got better and better, and it flowed faster and faster. I was struggling to keep up.

After about fifty pages, Ron announced that he wanted to finish it by the end of July.

"July?" I said, thinking, *"Even January seems way too soon."*

The story was finished on August 3, just three days beyond the end of July. If you had told me on June 3rd that this book would be written in 61 days... with no plan or outline... by a man who had barely read a book... a man who had never written anything before... I would not have believed it. But, here I am, staring in awe at these pages. So, I believe it now because, at least for me... *Seeing is believing.*

Muriel Lange

INTERVIEWER'S NOTE

Thoughts from Kathy

G od has a way of connecting people, bringing them together, and preparing them in a unique way that you recognize only later. The people I interviewed for this book reflected the way God had prepared them to respond and walk in faith as they played their parts in Patsy's miracle journey.

Bernie, Ron's sister made herself instantly available upon receiving Ron's initial call for help. Her steadfast presence and persistence kept Patsy from harm. Bernie was awed by the beauty of Ron's faith, both in his professional and his personal life. "He never gave up! He always got back up, dusted himself off, and kept on going." Bernie watched him grow in faith and become more connected in his walk with God.

God prepared Linda ahead of time by giving her the grace to take care of family members, thereby becoming a great caregiver and teacher for Patsy. God planted the seed for the wonderful friendship that grew between Patsy and Linda. I could hear the amazement in Linda's voice as she shared the story of Patsy's recovery with me, and I could sense the awe and wonder that she felt as Patsy worked to relearn everything again.

Ron "leaned on the shelter of the Most High" (Psalm 91:1). He looked beyond the grim diagnosis that the doctors offered, and rested in the promise that God had spoken to him. I absolutely believe that Ron heard God speak to Him because I have experienced it too as have many other Christians. Miracles are a way for God to shine a spotlight on the visible platform of His work in people's lives. His miracles call attention to Him as the Creator, Sustainer, and Lord of All. The hand of God was evident in the lives of all those I interviewed. Blessings to you all.

Kathy Puder

ACKNOWLEDGEMENTS

Thanks from Ron

First, I want to thank Kathy Puder for her efforts in interviewing the people who were part of this book. Her reports were thorough and concise, helping to jog my memory and to provide a check on the accuracy of details. Kathy was also very helpful as the third set of eyes proofreading this miracle story. Kathy is a writer and is now writing another children's Christmas book about Jesus. I love this girl like my daughter. Kathy's love and heart for Jesus are contagious, and it shows in her writing.

Next, I want to thank Muriel Lange for her outstanding editing that made me look like such a great writer. Muriel tutored me in a crash course in English grammar during the course of writing this book. Her efforts contributed greatly to my writing skills for this miracle story. She is also one of those women about whom you can say, "I am Woman, hear me roar." Muriel worked tirelessly day and night to meet the eight-week schedule I set for finishing this story. Her energy and intelligence are nothing less than God-sent. I have learned so much from Muriel. She is the teacher's teacher and is my candidate for teacher of the year. Thank you, Muriel, for all the patient teaching provided to Patsy over the last several years.

I want to thank Robert Ousnamer for his expertise in creating the beautiful cover design, for his patience in making the myriad changes I requested, and for his helpful advice on the title, subtitles and many other details. I also thank Christy Callahan for her attention to detail as she fact-checked and performed the final edit on this story. And I want to thank Cheri Cowell, the owner of EA Books Publishing, for providing topnotch staff to put the final touches on this book.

Last, I want to thank You, Jesus, for bringing Muriel into my life as well as Patsy's, and for using her to enhance Your words. Thank You, God, for Patsy's miracle and the healing of my marriage. Thank You for all the pushing You did to get me to the doctor to learn what deficiencies were holding me back from living my life and serving You to the fullest. Thank you, Lord, for giving me the grace to write this book.

Ron and Patsy appear on
the front page of the
July 11, 2007
edition of the
Atlanta Journal Constitution,
standing in front of one
of their nine
billboards.

ABOUT THE AUTHOR

Ron Tripodo started life with the disadvantage of severe ADHD, but with the blessing of a devoted mother who instilled in him the knowledge of God's love and the will to persevere. Despite his struggles with ADHD, Ron became a highly successful entrepreneur with five start-up companies to his credit as well as *Nite of Hope*, a non-profit for empowering the homeless.

More recently, Ron attended the John Maxwell Training Course, and, in 2016, he became a certified keynote speaker. He hints at the possibility of another book in the near future.

Ron lives in Woodstock, Georgia, with his wife, Patsy, and their two dogs, Willie Wonka and Winnie the Pooh.

Willie Wonka

Winnie the Pooh

Made in the
USA
Columbia, SC